French Communism and Local Power

For my family —
Julie, Jennifer and Wendy

French Communism and Local Power

Urban Politics and Political Change

Martin A. Schain

St. Martin's Press, New York

St. Martin's Press, Inc., 175 Fifth Avenue, New York, NY 10010
Printed in Great Britain
First published in the United States of America in 1985

Library of Congress Cataloging in Publication Data

Schain, Martin, 1940–
French Communism and local power.
Includes bibliographical references and index.
1. Communism—France. 2. Municipal government—France.
I. Title
HX269.S3 1985 320.8′0944 81-84035
ISBN 0-312-30445-5 AACR2

Contents

Acknowledgments

Many friends and colleagues contributed to my understanding of local government in France and to the role that Communists have played. Douglas Ashford, Jeannette Becquart-Leclercq and Donna Bahry read and commented on various parts of the manuscript of this book. Mark Kesselman and Philip Cerny also read and commented on parts of the manuscript, and our continual dialogue about French politics in conferences, colloquia and informal conversations has profoundly influenced my thinking. My association with the Institute of French Studies of New York University, and in particular with its director, Nicholas Wahl, has given me a unique opportunity to work out many of the ideas that I have developed in this book. My colleagues at the Institut d'Études Politiques in Paris, particularly Jean-Louis Quermonne and Georges Lavau, have been generous with their time and supportive with their contacts, and Communist and Socialist local officials, too numerous to mention by name, have given me a great deal of their time and their unique insights into problems of local government in France. Without these people, this study would not have been possible. Of course, I alone am responsible for the analysis and conclusions in this book. I count myself lucky to have a stimulating network of colleagues in the United States, England and France. I also count myself lucky to have a loving and supportive family, who have shared with me the pleasures as well as the problems of field research and writing.

1 Communism and Local Government in France

Introduction

This study was undertaken to answer some simple, but generally neglected questions about Communists and government in France. Most of what has been written about French Communists focuses on their role as the principal opposition during the last sixty years to three republics. The party itself has been seen as a permanent and principalled opposition, and electoral support for the party has been seen as a manifestation of mass protest and alienation. Supported by dissatisfied, deprived and alienated voters, the attractiveness of the party has been related more to its implacable anti-regime opposition than to its revolution vocation.[1]

However, Communists have also held government responsibility in France. The French Communist Party (the PCF) participated in tripartite coalition governments from 1944 to 1947, and was part of the left coalition governing France from June 1981, to 1 July 1984. The most enduring experience of the PCF with governmental power, however, has been at the local level. Beginning with the municipal elections of 1925, Communists have governed in a network of cities and towns in France.[2] During the Fifth Republic, until 1983 in the larger towns (those with greater than 30,000 population), Communists maintained and increased the number of local governments that they controlled. They participated in the coalition governments of almost two-thirds of the larger towns, and were the mayors in almost one-third. The phenomenon of Communist government is neither new nor rare, and, at least at the local level, the PCF is well established as a party in power. Communists have had a stable and developing pattern of support; they are identified with patterns of policy choices; and they have had a characteristic process of governing and making policy.

The questions with which this study is concerned involve the role that Communists play in government at the local level: the way that they develop support, the policy choices that they make, and the processes and structures through which they govern. The focus is not on the party, but on the network of local governments with Communist mayors, particularly those in towns with populations greater than 30,000. While the party is an important element of Communist government, we will examine Communists as makers of policy, rather than positions, as established authority, rather than opposition to established authority, and as mobilizers of support for governments (their own), rather than against government. This is far from a complete picture of Communism in France, but it is an aspect of the Communist phenomenon that has been largely ignored, except for a handful of case studies.[3] This analysis of government at the local level will permit us to gain a different perspective on the bases for Communist support, and will offer the possibility of a somewhat different interpretation of the exercise of local power in France, derived from the Communist experience. To analyze Communist local government, however, we must first examine the limitations and the conditions of local power in France.

Formal restrictions on the exercise of local power

The formal restrictions on the activities of local governments in France have been substantial. The central state, through the prefects, has regularly monitored the legality of the activities of local officials, as well as the 'wisdom and desirability' of most of their undertakings.[4] Communes have been obliged to do certain things, forbidden to do others, and, in a limited number of cases, they have been required to receive prior approval of the prefect before an activity could be undertaken.

Thus, communes have been obliged to submit a balanced budget and to pay debts to which they are committed. When these obligations were not fulfilled by action of the municipal council, the municipal code provides they they could be fulfilled by the prefect.[5] The mayor, as a representative of the administration and as an officer of the *police judiciaire*, has been obliged 'to assure order, safety, security and the public salubrity.'[6] If, however, the mayor either refused or neglected these obligations, the prefect could impose his own authority. In each case, administrative authority could be substituted for locally elected authority. In addition, certain specific acts by a municipality could be annulled by the prefect when he judged them to be contrary to law, beyond the competence of the municipal government, or when he concluded that a member of the municipal council was an interested party in a decision. Administrative power to annul or suspend decisions also applied to police regulations issued by the mayor.[7]

These direct administrative controls over the activities of locally elected officials have been exercised in exceptional cases, since they ordinarily have been the basis of bargaining between prefects and mayors. For example, the Prefect of the Somme pointed out that in his department in 1975 only two decisions by local councils were annulled, and Yves Mény notes that 'at the national level the figures given in a debate in Parliament are of the same order.' Thus, the abandonment of the formal administrative *tutelle* in the *loi Defferre* in 1982 generally reaffirmed the existing process, but removed a symbolic irritant. The prefect (now renamed the commissioner of the republic) can bring local governments before administrative tribunal if he believes that a local decision is illegal, but this 'merely formalizes *a posteriori* something which occurred *a priori* informally and often at the request of the mayor himself.'[8]

There are also categories of decisions that have required the specific approval of the prefect before they could take effect. These categories were significantly reduced in the years before 1981, particularly for smaller towns, and the items that remained dealt primarily with the financial transactions of the commune: accounts that were out of balance, loans that were contracted by the municipality from private agencies, guarantees given to private agencies for loans, taxes imposed above a fixed level, certain municipal salaries and industrial and commercial ventures undertaken by the commune.[9] In these cases, the decision of the prefect was not based simply on legality, but on desirability as well.[10]

Finally, beyond direct and indirect administrative supervision, local authorities have been obliged to operate within a plethora of administrative 'decrees' and 'circulars' that set national standards for everything from the construction of housing to the noise levels of traffic on streets and highways.[11] Thus national standards have imposed extensive formal barriers to local decision-making and have limited the range of local choices. While the rules for imposing such standards have now been changed, the pressures to impose them are not likely to decline.[12]

Nevertheless, even before the post-1981 decentralization legislation, there remained an arena within which local discretion could be effectively exercised. French communes retained broad powers of regulation and initiative, ranging from film censorship to the organization and construction of urban renewal projects.[13] They could choose to provide numerous municipal services such as day-care centers, free public transportation and summer camps, and they could supplement such services provided by the central state as public welfare and public education. Perhaps most important, communes were largely responsible for taking the initiative in large urban renewal projects as well as more limited public construction such as new school buildings, sports facilities and low-income housing.[14]

Local governments have become increasingly important since the Second World War as arenas of economic activity, particularly public investment. In 1972, the investment money spent by localities was almost half of all public investment, a proportion almost double that of the United Kingdom. During the 1970s, local authorities were responsible for 60 percent of all public works projects (*équipement*) in France.[15] The proportion of these projects sponsored by town government increased steadily during the decade of the 1970s.[16]

What does this mean, however, in terms of local power? In order to finance their investments, communes have burdened themselves with increasingly greater debts. In 1973, 53 percent of the cost of the investments made by the communes came from loans, mostly from state banks, while they were able to pay for less than a third of their investment spending out of their own revenues. Between 1959 and 1980 the proportion of public investment paid for by local governments increased from 56 to 75 percent.[17] French scholars and legal theorists have generally argued that financial dependence on the central state has meant that as formal administrative control has been eased, it has been replaced by a more subtle, but no less effective, financial control — the establishment of criteria and the ordering of local priorities through loans and grants.[18] Others (generally American), on the other hand, have argued that the volume of local investment can also mean a dependence of the central state on local decision-making for the fulfillment of key national objectives.[19]

The point is, of course, that formal administrative barriers, and the remaining local arena of decision-making and discretion, provide the context within which local power is developed. The questions, then, are: How effective is central control in practice? How effective is the power of local government authorities? And how has it been used?

Institutional arrangements and the conditions of local power

Within the constraints of administrative controls and financial dependency, local authorities have developed considerable political power. This power becomes more evident if we conceptualize power in relational terms, as well as in terms of local autonomy: the power to resist the central state, to influence decisions made by the state, and to innovate and initiate policy at the local level.[20] Studies that focus on institutional arrangements generally tend to discount local power because they emphasize the more formal aspects of local autonomy. Studies of the decision-making and policy process, on the other hand, which examine relational power, have brought the conditions necessary for local power into sharper focus.

For example, Jean de Savigny, in a highly regarded book published in 1971, analyzes the contradiction between the increasingly vast array of functions performed by communes (*la commune providence*) and the limitations on local decision-making increasingly imposed by the central state. According to Savigny, there is practically no communal activity that is not the object of regulation, and the range of autonomous local decision-making authority has probably narrowed as the obligations of the communes have expanded.[21]

Studies of center–periphery relations, that have analyzed and examined the complexity of the political-administrative structure and process, have concluded, however, that local power (even as autonomy) remains considerable, and the ability of the central state to impose its will is limited. These studies present a different picture of the effective power of administrative centralization in France, and bring into question the assumption that local governments essentially carry out central decisions, that variations in local decision-making are unimportant, and that local institutions have little impact on central administration control.[22] Charles Riog, for example, cautioned in 1966 that we should be wary of overly formalistic views of administrative regulation in France. 'Decentralization . . . is not merely the margin of formal liberty left to local officials: it also includes the liberty of action that local officials achieve by interpreting, evading or ignoring the texts . . .'[23]

Central control is clearly conditional, they argue, and power is dispersed within the administrative command structure. Compared with other centralized systems, France may be far less centralized in terms of the actual ability of the center to dominate the periphery, particularly in terms of policy-making, than we have usually assumed. Douglas Ashford concludes that 'in functional terms, the dominance of the Whitehall cadre over local affairs [in Britain] may be much greater than that of the French bureaucracy. In this respect, Britain is more centralized than France.'[24]

The process that is described in the recent literature suggests that there are several key conditions that determine (or at least support) variations in the ability of local governments in France to develop local power. The most important of these conditions is access to the administrative structure. While under the formal *tutelle* of the state, local officials have enhanced their political power, to protect their autonomy and effectively bargain with the administration, by exploiting mutual dependency and by modifying the structural isolation of local government.

The field representatives of the administration need the mayors to facilitate the acceptance of the authority of the state, and to provide information without which they cannot operate effectively at the local level. They also need the cooperation of the mayors for initiating numerous projects that can only be recommended by the administration.[25] For the mayors, cooperation with the administrative field services provides the possibility for acting as privileged conduits between the communes and the state. Special access enables a mayor to accomplish the objectives of his government more easily, to protect his commune in the implementation of national policy, to deal more effectively with individual requests of his constituents, and to solidify local support.

> The mayor is, for the population, the individual charged with promoting the interests of the commune higher in the system. The best mayor is not the one who can accomplish the most, or who is politically the most seductive; it is the individual who has the best network of access with those who count in the department or in Paris.[26]

Privileged access is frequently reinforced by the French tradition of *cumul des mandats*, which permits one person to hold several political offices at different levels of government at the same time. Mayors and municipal councilors (particularly those of larger towns) are often members of the departmental general council, as well as members of the National Assembly or the Senate. In the National Assembly elected in 1978, 68 percent of the deputies were either mayors or municipal councilors, and 61 percent were departmental general councilors. Only 17 percent held no local office. The percentages for the Assembly elected in 1981 are similar. In the Senate, fewer than 7 percent held no local office.[27] *Cumul des mandats* often enables mayors to bypass the field services of the central administration entirely, and to gain access directly to central decision-makers.

Thus, either through mutual dependency with the field services, through direct access to decision-makers at the center, or both, local officials have developed the power to resist, to bargain and to initiate. With proper access, local governments can effectively modify and even veto decisions made by the central state. However, connections are most essential for attempts to innovate and to initiate new projects.[28] In this sense, we are told that local power varies directly with access. It is not surprising, then, that Crozier and Thoenig found that mayors frequently see the administrative field service as allies rather than adversaries, and that mayors who are multiple office holders most frequently reject the adversary view. (See Table 1.1.)

Table 1.1

Which of these two sentences appears to you to best reflect the mentality of the administration in the department?

	When they can, they do not hesitate to defend local interests against Paris.	They do what Paris tells them to do, without worrying too much about local interests.
Mayors with one or more other elected offices (% agreeing)	91	9
Mayors not holding any other elected office (% agreeing)	60	40

Source: Michel Crozier and J-C. Thoenig, 'La Regulation des systèmes organisés complexes,' *Revue Française de Sociologie*, January-March, 1975, p. 1.

Mayors of larger towns are more likely to have accumulated offices, which enhances their access to central decision-makers.[29] However, the direct access of mayors of larger towns appears to be considerable, whether or not they are multiple office holders, and their dependence on the services offered by the administrative field services is minimized by the availability of municipal services and resources. For this reason, they often play a mediation role for other local elected officials, and a more important role in center–periphery bargaining than other mayors. Howard Machin contends that these mayors are so powerful, that it is a mistake to try to understand their role in terms of mutual dependency or cross-regulation.[30] In addition to their political advantage, mayors of larger towns are likely to have the 'sociological advantage' of coming from backgrounds similar to those of the administrators with whom they deal. Thus, according to data presented by Pierre Birnbaum, almost half the mayors before 1983 in towns with populations greater than 30,000 were either industrialists, higher level managers or top civil servants.[31]

The bargaining power of all communal governments is increased by several other political conditions that tend to strengthen their internal cohesion. Between 1965 and 1983, the electoral law that governed communal elections in cities with over 30,000 population (with the exception of Paris, Lyon, Marseilles and Bordeaux) helped to minimize the institutionalized expression of opposition at the local level. In the process of *scrutin de liste majoritaire à deux tours*, lists with a number of candidates equal to the required number of seats competed in local elections. A list that received more than 50 percent of the votes in the first round, or a plurality in the second round, gained all of the seats in the municipal council. The council then elected the mayor, who was normally the head of the list. Lists could not be changed between rounds, and a voter can only cast a ballot for a complete list. Thus, in most of the larger towns in France, there was no formal opposition to the municipal council between 1965 and 1983.

This consequence of the electoral law was supported by a more widespread pattern of consensus-building in French local government that existed independently of electoral legislation. Even without the encouragement of the electoral law, the governments of most French communes (even those in which the council was elected by proportional representation, and which therefore guaranteed representation to the opposition) have worked hard to minimize opposition by presenting balanced lists that frequently have included former opponents. While this process has been most characteristic of smaller towns, it also has not been unusual in larger towns.[32] In smaller towns, where political opponents *are* elected to the municipal council, they tend to 'disappear' after the election; that is, opposition itself tends to disappear.[33]

In larger towns that elected Communist–Socialist majorities in 1977, often in hard-fought, bitter contests, every mayor and assistant mayor interviewed affirmed that he confronted no important organized opposition to the new government within the commune after the election. From time to time there have been sharp conflicts within the left coalitions, but in no case did the center or right opposition maintain an effective, organized presence within the commune. Newspaper reports on conflicts that have periodically erupted within the left coalitions have consistently treated them as exceptional, rather than the normal interactions of day-to-day governing.

Local governments in France are also strengthened politically by the cohesiveness of their structures, and by their ability to resist domination by organized private interests. In contrast to the United States, where political authority in cities is often highly fragmented, and where pressure groups frequently play a key role in determining urban policy, French mayors (and their assistant mayors) tend to dominate political life, and local interest groups are peripheral to the political process.[34]

Thus, the bargaining power of localities, particularly larger towns, can be considerable. The effectiveness of local power to resist the central state, to influence decisions made by the state, and to initiate policy is most evident in studies of policy development and policy implementation.

Jerry Webman, looking at decision-making in urban redevelopment projects in Lyon, sees a complex of interdependent decisions among government levels, rather than simple control by one level or the other in the making of policy.

> Because different agencies at different levels of government could intervene to advance their different concerns at any point in the course of a program, projects [of redevelopment] were subject to change, compromise, and minimalist strategies. No agency had the political ability to design a plan, finance it, and impose it, and no one's plan was ever implemented.[35]

Webman's analysis is supported by a decision-making study by Octave Gélinier. Gélinier analyzes fourteen interrelated decision-makers at four governmental levels, involving four ministries that are concerned with a decision to build a high school.[36] French intergovernmental relations, as presented by Webman and Gélinier, seem far closer to the interdependent/veto model usually associated with the American political process, than to the command structure associated with the French system.[37]

Other studies have focused on the important policy initiatives, choices and responsibilities of local authorities that are revealed in the policy process. Louis Bériot concludes that:

> For decades we have had to listen to jeremiades about the authoritarian central administration, a discretionary, blind monster ... Too many examples [however] attest to the position of influence of local elected officials on the evolution of their city or village; too many examples that permit us to reprimand those who have let their commune be devoured by speculators, destroyed by ideologies of growth ... If we are to believe the complaints of the mayors, how can we explain, for example, that the commune of Git-sur-Yvette in the Essonne — the department in France most subject to land-value pressures — has been able to buy one-quarter of its territory in 18 years ... that Tours preserved its city-center, while maintaining a commitment to bring in a diverse population and low income housing, while Paris preserves [its center-city] for the most privileged classes ... or that Metz, under the administration of its former mayor was determined to bulldoze everything.[38]

While Bordeaux, Toulouse, Lyon, Marseilles, Saint-Denis and Argenteuil chose *croissance dévorante* (all-consuming growth), according to Bériot, Rennes, Nice and Annecy mastered urban expansion and controlled urban sprawl. It is not appropriate to blame the problems of urban development on priorities established and pushed by the central state, argues Bériot. All decision-makers must assume responsibility for the mistakes that have been made.[39]

Even when local officials have operated within the constraints of national standards set by the ministries in Paris, the standards themselves may reflect local influence at the national level. 'Very often the center, in issuing circulars determining minimum standards, is only responding to the wishes of local councils themselves.'[40]

Thus, numerous studies indicate that policy development can be understood as an interdependent process, in which there are real choices that have been made at the local level, and in which local governments have had substantial influence in bargaining with the state. In this context, the decentralization reforms initiated by the national government after 1981 both formalize this interdependence and somewhat alter its form. The broad range of initiatives actually undertaken by local governments have been given legislative recognition, while the bargaining relationship that had developed between elected and administrative authorities was liberated from the remnants of administrative *tutelle*.

Decentralization legislation generally enshrines and augments and encourages actions on the land use regulation and the economic initiatives that many local governments have been exercising for many years. Mayors now have the right to issue building permits (formerly issued by the prefect), and have gained expanded prerogatives to subsidize, support and stimulate local economic activity (modelled on the many practices of Gaston Defferre in Marseilles and Pierre Mauroy in Lille).[41] While decentralization has created new possibilities for urban initiative, in general it reaffirms the past practices of activist mayors. However, if the autonomy of local initiative has been strengthened, policy initiatives have also been encouraged at the department level, as well as on the regional level. The most obvious changes in the decentralization legislation are the new powers of initiative that have been given to the departments to build schools, regulate welfare, facilitate economic development, provide technical assistance to localities and the development and regulation of social services.

Since departmental executive functions have now been transferred from the prefect to the president of the departmental council, the hands of those mayors who also serve on departmental councils have clearly been strengthened in the network of interdependence, a reaffirmation, as Yves Mény has argued, that 'in the struggle between the "boss" (the mayor) and the "manager" (the prefect) it is the former who, during the past two decades, has got the better of the latter who has now been downgraded from the prestigious title of prefect to the more prosaic *Commissaire de la République*.'[42] However, interdependence for successful initiatives remains the rule, and, indeed, may have been made far more complex by decentralization. In this sense the possibility of local autonomous action may have been reduced.

'The somewhat distant *tutelle* of the state' has been replaced for some mayors 'by the potentially more constricting stewardship of the department and/or region,' and there has been an increase in the number of actors involved in the decision-making process.[43] In no policy area has an intermediate level of government acquired full functional control, and, therefore, interdependence among levels of decision-makers has become more important and more complex than ever. These consequences of decentralization had begun to emerge during the Giscard years. A 1976 study of the impact of administrative deconcentration under Giscard found that for a decision involving local investment, the number of decisions required in Paris had been reduced from seven to five (the number of ministries involved had been reduced from four to two), but three regional and six departmental decision-makers had been added; thus, through deconcentration the number of decision-makers had doubled, the complexity in terms of coordination had quadrupled, and the possibility of a successful completion of the process had diminished.[44] Gary Meyers found that, in addition to the growing administrative complexity under Giscard, political complexity accentuated by Socialist decentralization diminished the effective ability of the former Socialist government of Grenoble to gain benefits from the state.[45] Far from transferring different policy functions to different levels of government, decentralization has accentuated the previous tendency towards complexity.[46]

The decentralization legislation does appear to provide new opportunities for local governments to initiate and innovate. In order to understand the importance of these opportunities, however, it is important to understand how more restricted power was used by local authorities before 1981. French researchers have noted that there were wide variations in the way that local prerogatives were used. According to numerous studies, policy innovations and initiatives were frequently avoided in just those localities where conditions seemed to be most favorable.[47] The cautious use of positive power has been related to the fear of mayors that innovation could undermine the foundations upon which their local support was built. What Mark Kesselman has called the 'rhetoric of *apolitisme*' is, in part, a strategy of governing by minimizing local conflict and avoiding issues upon which opposition can be built. Although innovation has sometimes been unavoidable, and

> Whilst within his circumscribed commune the mayor's capacity to innovate is greater than that of any elected person other than the president of the republic, he seldom does innovate because he places the harmony of the community above all other purposes and fears that change will be disruptive. His leadership is therefore passive in character, except in the larger towns where developments beyond his control compel him to sponsor innovation.[48]

The basic strategy for building support has been for a mayor to respond to requests for help from interests and individuals on a personal and piecemeal basis.

This approach has been linked to the general weakness of party organization, and the lack of coordination between party and government at the local level. Crozier and Friedberg found that 'local decisions escape the conditioning of administrative organizations,' while Jack Hayward argued that the lack of such 'conditioning' lead 'to the direct regulations between the executive [the mayor] and the many supplicants for its favours.'[49] Although branches of the national political parties may be established at the local level, 'the political parties have other interests . . .' and perform no important role either in establishing local priorities or in linking the center to the periphery.[50]

Decentralization has certainly increased the importance of political actors in the network of decision-making. Elected officials, particularly presidents of the departmental councils, have benefited from the reforms, both because of the transfer of executive functions from the prefect to the council president, and because of the transfer of bureaucratic support.[51] Thus, the ascendancy of the political 'bosses' referred to by Mény is reaffirmed and augmented. However, recent literature gives no clear indication that the 'conditioning' of political parties has been strengthened at the local level. The ability of political parties to influence and condition the priorities of local governments is related to their ability to control political actors.

Gary Meyers found that for Grenoble, the Socialist Party

became an arena of conflict after 1981, within which the local government competed for policy advantages. The more complex relations of power under decentralized procedures reduced the bargaining power of the local authorities but did not increase the influence of political parties over policy. While Grenoble was relatively favored under right-wing governments because of its well-developed administrative network, it '. . . was forced to compete openly for funding with a large number of other *municipalités de gauche* after May, 1981' for state funding. In addition, the former Socialist mayor, Dubedout, had been strongly identified with the Rocard wing of the party, and, therefore, local government officials felt that they were not favored by Socialists at the department level allied with Mitterrand.[52] This pattern was confirmed by a subprefect appointed by an opposition general council president to direct the departmental bureaucracy, interviewed by Mark Kesselman. He '. . . admitted the reform might provoke a scramble for influence among local politicians, with decisions made wholly on the basis of power relations rather than equitable criteria.'[53]

In general, local power, even in larger towns, has been used to resist the imposition of policy from the center and to promote, piecemeal, the interests of individual constituents and groups. The considerable possibility to initiate and innovate has been used sparingly, reflecting the conservative political strategy of most municipal governments. This pattern would be the least likely to change under decentralization.

Of course there is variation, particularly in the larger towns (As Bériot emphasizes), but variation is usually related to the objectives, skills and access of individual mayors. Nevertheless, a few studies have demonstrated quite clearly that higher levels of policy initiation and innovation are associated with a left partisan orientation, although for any given level of policy outputs, access of the left to the administrative network was less extensive and advantageous than that of the right before 1981.[54]

The Communist pattern

The problem with the foregoing analysis of local power in

France is that it virtually ignores localities governed by Communists. In studies of local government, the Communist cases are treated as exotic exceptions, while in case studies of Communist local government there have been few attempts to relate the findings to more general considerations of local politics in France.[55]

> But paradoxically, while 9 million Frenchmen [in 1983] live today in these [Communist-governed] communes, while numerous specialists are in agreement in their recognition that the strength of the PCF is largely found in its local implantation, the world of research and of the university is not interested in this phenomenon ... Another paradox, if dozens, even hundreds of books have appeared to clarify the PCF from within, not one has yet focused essentially on the municipalities of the party. A veritable law of silence seems to be imposed, stronger than the one that reigns within the national directorate [of the party].[56]

Scholars have not completely ignored Communist governments at the local level. However, they have generally analyzed them as a phenomenon that is separate and apart from other local governments in France. There appears to be a working assumption that Communist-governed towns are both different from others and similar to one another. Thus, even if 'local decisions escape the conditioning of political organizations' in other towns, this is obviously not true in towns governed by Communists.

'Communes headed by Communist mayors are classified as the best run and best-equipped in France,' Crozier and Thoenig mention in passing.[57] Other studies before 1983 referred to a higher level of efficiency, greater honesty and a more activist orientation in the initiation of local improvements as the chief characteristics of Communist government at the local level.[58] The few case studies that we have conclude that Communists are not only different in what they do when they govern at the local level, but they are also different in how they govern and how they attract support. Thus, Communists govern in an 'openly partisan manner,' they are 'both capable and persistent, and as a result, probably receive more state aid than any comparable group of French mayors,' despite comparatively poor access to the political-administrative system.[59] In fact, very little attention has been given to how Communist local governments generate power within the system. Support, on the other hand, has been frequently attributed to the ability of Communist governments to deliver in terms of policy, to their ability to answer the 'bread and butter interests of their clientele.'[60] In contrast to other municipalities, they build support on openly partisan government and policy outputs.

Communist local governments, therefore, present us with a different pattern of governing, a different pattern for generating support within the system, and a different way of building local electoral support. However, the Communist pattern is frequently discounted because it is seen as a unique aspect of a working-class subculture, and because the phenomenon itself is seen as quite limited. Moreover, Communist local government is understood as more relevant for an understanding of the operation of the French Communist Party than for an understanding of local politics and local power. Nevertheless, there are good reasons to believe that this judgment is wrong.

The roots of Communist local government are in the working-class subculture of the 'red belt' of Paris.[61] However, for some time, Communists have attracted support at the local level that goes well beyond this core. By 1981, 42 percent of the seventy-two larger towns with Communist mayors were in the provinces, and only 14 percent had a majority working-class population. Furthermore, during the Fifth Republic, when the Communists were expanding their presence at the local level, the absolute number of blue-collar workers, as well as the relative concentrations of workers, was diminishing. (See below, Chapter 2.) Thus, although Communist mayors still governed in working-class suburbs of Paris such as Saint-Denis, Ivry and Vitry, until 1983, they also governed in Arles and Nîmes, two southern cities with extensive Roman ruins and few workers, as well as Antony, a Paris suburb with few workers but large numbers of professionals and intellectuals. While there are important political differences between Communist-governed cities and those governed by other parties — differences that we will explore throughout this study — they are no longer demographically distinct as working-class towns; indeed, working-class towns are becoming increasingly rare.

Moreover, the phenomenon of Communist local government is no longer exceptional in the sense that it is limited, even after the electoral losses of 1983. As a proportion of the more than 36,000 communes in France, Communist-governed communes have always been unusual. In 1981, Communists participated in only 3 percent of the local governments in France, and were mayors in only 2.5 percent. However, these percentages are somewhat deceptive. In the larger towns, those with more than 30,000 population, where 35 percent of the population live, Communist presence is strong and even dominant. Among the 229 larger towns, they were mayors in seventy-two, and participated in coalition governments in another sixty-nine before 1983. Communists have been well established in local government for over sixty years, and from 1959 until 1983 their presence expanded, especially in the larger towns.[62] Communist office holders are also well integrated into the structure of local national *political* linkages. Almost two-thirds of the Communist deputies elected in 1978 were elected municipal officials (a proportion comparable to other major parties), and a quarter of their mayors of larger towns won seats in the National Assembly in 1978. In 1981, more than half of the Communist deputies elected were mayors (about the same as other parties). Thus, the phenomenon of Communist local government is neither marginal nor transitory, and it represents a substantial part of the experience of local government in France.

The importance of a network of local governments for the Communist Party is not always clear. Of course, local electoral victories have always had value as a symbol of the extent and depth of party support, and the local election process and local government have provided an arena within which national strategies have been tested. The municipalities have also provided the possibility of building a stable following 'for use in offensive and defensive strategy.' (See Chapter 2, pp. 32–3.)

While the municipalities have served the party (and indeed Pronier's recent study refers to the 'municipalisation' of the PCF), a one-sided analysis is too limited. Communist-governed towns are analyzed as if they operate in an entirely different context from other towns in France. It is the party context that defines the role of the local government, and it is within this context that the actions of the local governments are understood. Whatever role the municipalities have had in serving the goals of the party, however, not all objectives pursued at the local level can be related to changing party strategy and goals. Over the years, local government has developed a life and importance of its own.

What is missing in the study of local government in France is an analysis and integration of the Communist experience, and what is missing in the study of Communism in France is an analysis of the Communist experience of governing day to day. Based upon the few existing case studies of Communist-governed municipalities, it appears that the Communist experience *is* conditioned by political organization, and in that sense it is different from that of other municipalities, even those characterized by similar processes and policy patterns. In their ability to get loans and grants from the state, to develop their own service and public works programs and their own policy priorities, while maintaining high levels of electoral support, Communist local governments have also demonstrated that there may be different strategies for gaining necessary financial support from the state, building stable electoral support, and linking the two. In a world in which the rhetoric of *apoliticisme*, access and the avoidance of policy choices have been related to state aid and political support, Communist local governments have operated differently and have been successful.

An understanding of the Communist pattern of local government, and the strategy their local officials have used to develop the power to resist the central state, to influence decisions made by the state and to innovate and initiate policies at the local level, will deepen our understanding of what Communist government has meant, and broaden our understanding of the power and possibilities of local government in France. An understanding of the evolution of Communist local government can also help us to understand the decline of national and local electoral support from which the PCF has suffered since 1981. Indeed, we will argue that the very success of building a more complex social and political basis for local political support has carried with it the danger of electoral decline.

We will examine the pattern from several different points of view. First we will look at the changing bases of support for Communist local government, and analyze some of the existing explanations for their ability to gain and maintain governmental power. We will then examine the question of whether governmental power by Communists makes any difference in policy terms; if it does, can these differences be explained by ideological commitments alone, or can we also find explanations in differences in the structure of government and the process of policy-making in Communist-governed municipalities? We will find that the Communist experience supports the hypothesis, developed in much of the existing literature, that local policy outputs must be understood in terms of extra-local linkages, but suggests that these linkages are also related to the local political process as well as to changing patterns of support. Moreover, the linkages important in the Communist case are not simply administrative, but political as well — the national PCF and interparty relations. If the administrative network involves 'cross regulation' and interdependence, the political network is also complex and interdependent.

This study is based on a broad range of data drawn from the seventy-two towns with populations greater than 30,000 that have Communist mayors. Electoral, budget and policy data have been supplemented with interviews concentrated in nine towns that elected new Communist mayors in 1977 and five towns having Communist mayors for longer periods of time. On this basis, we intend to carry our analysis beyond the few monographs that have been written on this subject.[63]

Notes

1. See Chapter 2, pp. 24–35.
2. Precise figures on the number of towns governed by Communists are difficult to find. From the available figures, however, it appears that by the Second World War there were just over 300 Communist-governed towns. In provisional elections just after the liberation in 1944, the number rose to over 1,400, but was greatly reduced in 1947. During the Fifth Republic, the number has slowly, but steadily, increased until 1983. In 1981, there were about 1,500 cities and towns with Communist mayors. For details, see Chapter 2.

3. See Georges Lavau, *A quoi sert le parti communiste français?* (Paris: Fayard, 1981), p. 312, n. 1; and Raymond Pronier, *Les Municipalités Communistes* (Paris: Balland, 1983).
4. See Mark Kesselman, *The Ambiguous Consensus* (New York: Knopf, 1967), Appendix B, pp. 171–84.
5. Jacques Moreau, *Administration régionale, locale et municipale* (Paris: Dalloz, 1972), p. 24; *Code de l'administration communale* (hereafter cited as *CM*) (Paris: Éditions Berger-Livrault, 1973), Articles 174–84.
6. *CM*, Articles 77, 78, 96, 97.
7. Ibid., Articles 42–6 and 82; Moreau, op. cit., p. 25.
8. Yves Mény, 'Decentralisation in Socialist France: The Politics of Pragmatism,' *West European Politics*, 7, No. 1, January 1984, p. 70.
9. *CM*, Articles 47–9.
10. Moreau, op. cit., p. 26.
11. See, for example, 'Pour les villes sans bruit,' *Projet*, **155**, May, 1981.
12. Mény, op. cit., p. 76.
13. Kesselman, op. cit., pp. 181–2; and Roger Aubin, *Communes et democratie*, Vol. I (Paris: Éditions Ouvrières, 1965), p. 389.
14. Aubin, op. cit., Chs. II and III.
15. *Vivre ensemble, annexes au rapport de la commision de développement des responsabilités locales* (Paris: La Documentation Française, 1976), p. 80; and Douglas Ashford, ed., *Financing Urban Government in the Welfare State* (New York: St. Martin's Press, 1980), p. 16.
16. See the figures cited by Yves Mény in 'Financial Transfers and Local Government in France: National Policy Despite 36,000 Communes,' Ashford, op. cit., p. 151.
17. *Vivre ensemble, annexes*, p. 190; J. Cathelineau, 'Local Government Finance in France,' in Jacques Lagroye and Vincent Wright, eds, *Local Government in Britain and France* (London: George Allen and Unwin, 1979), p. 195; and Commission du Bilan, *La France en mai 1981*, 5, *L'État et les citoyens* (Paris: La Documentation Française, 1981), p. 270. The proportion varied from sector to sector: 86.1 percent of the total investment in sports and socio-educational facilities to 9.8 percent for public health. See F. de Lavergne, *Économie politique des équipements collectifs* (Paris: Economica, 1979), cited in Edmond Preteceille 'Left-wing Local Governments and Services Policy in France,' *International Journal of Urban and Regional Research*, **5**, No. 3, 1981, p. 411.
18. Moreau, op. cit., pp. 23–8; and Mény, 'Financial Transfers ...,' pp. 152–6.
19. Ashford, *Financing Urban Government*, p. 16; and Jerry A. Webman, 'Centralization and Implementation: Urban Renewal in Great Britain and France,' *Comparative Politics*, **13**, No. 2, January, 1981.
20. On the importance of linkages for the understanding of local power, see Jeanne Becquart-Leclerq, 'Relational Power and Center–Periphery Linkages in French Local Polity,' *Sociology and Social Research*, **62**, No. 1, October, 1977, pp. 21–42; and Mark Kesselman, 'Research Perspectives in Comparative Local Politics,' in Terry Clark, ed., *Comparative Community Politics* (Beverly Hills: Sage, 1974).

21. Jean de Savigny, *L'État contre les communes?* (Paris: Éditions du Seuil, 1971), pp. 35–9 and 46–54. For Savigny, however, this phenomenon is not limited to France. Less formalized central control 'is created by new procedures because of the exigencies of the modern state.' (p. 54). On this question, see Theodore Lowi, 'The Europeanization of America? From United States to One State,' in Theodore Lowi and Alan Stone, eds, *Nationalizing Government: Public Policies in America* (Beverly Hills: Sage Publications, 1978). While some of the new obligations undertaken by local governments in France have been imposed (or encouraged) by the state, others certainly represent a broader scope of local initiative.
22. Some of the earliest writing is reviewed in Stanley Hoffman, 'Areal Division of Power in the Writing of French Political Thinkers,' in Arthur Maas, *Area and Power: A Theory of Local Government* (Glencoe: Free Press, 1959), p. 139. More recent work is summarized by Howard Machin, 'Center and Periphery,' in Philip Cerny and Martin A. Schain, *French Politics and Public Policy* (London and New York: Frances Pinter, St. Martin's Press and Methuen University Paperbacks, 1980), pp. 125–40. The impact of the studies cited in this chapter can be seen in the treatment of local politics in the chapters on France in the second edition of Beer and Ulam, *Patterns of Government* (New York: Random House, 1962), by Nicholas Wahl, compared with the parallel chapters in the third edition (1973) by Suzanne Berger. Wahl writes (in 1962):

    > Although ... township or municipal councils (*conseils municipaux*) do exist, the serious decisions of local government policy are made by the prefect in consultation with his ministry or another Paris authority. [p. 450]

    Compare this to the parallel text by Berger:

    > From an administrative chart, it would appear that since local political authorities are under control of the prefect, he could marshall them to whatever ends he chose, just as a general can move around troops under his command. The reality of local politics is quite different ... the success of most of the prefect's plans depend on cooperation of ... communes. [p. 448]

23. Charles Riog, 'Théorie et réalité de la décentralisation,' *Revue Française de Science Politique*, January, 1966, p. 464.
24. Douglas Ashford, 'Are Britain and France Unitary?' *Comparative Politics*, July, 1977, p. 489.
25. See Kesselman, *Ambiguous Consensus*, pp. 62–3; Jean-Pierre Worms, 'Le Préfet et ses notables,' *Sociologie du Travail*, July, 1966, p. 250; Pierre Gremion, *Le Pouvoir périphérique* (Paris: Seuil, 1976), p. 303; and Jean-Claude Thoenig, 'Local Government Institutions and the Contemporary Evolution of French Society,' in Lagroye and Wright, op. cit., pp. 91–3.
26. Michel Crozier and Erhard Friedberg, *L'Acteur et le système* (Paris: Seuil, 1977), p. 228.
27. *Le Monde*, March 22, 1978; Alain Guede and Gilles Fabre Rosane, 'Portrait robot du député 1978,' *Le Matin de Paris*, April 19, 1978; Michel Reydillet, 'Le Cumul des mandats,' *Revue du Droit Publique et de la Science Politique*, No. 3, 1979, p. 729; *Le Monde*, August 8, 1981.

28. Jeannette Becquart-Leclercq, *Paradoxes du pouvoir local* (Paris: Presses de la FNSP, 1976), p. 205.
29. Thoenig has argued that 'The accumulation of offices is not a disease within the system, but an essential mechanism for its functioning. The representative who holds a number of offices offers the possibility of a more direct communication and a greater suppleness (J-C. Thoenig, 'Local Government Institutions,' p. 103, n. 33).
30. Machin, 'Center and Periphery,' p. 140. I am not convinced by Machin's argument. While mayors of large towns are certainly less dependent and regulated than those of smaller towns, it appears that this is a matter of degree. 'No local [political] leader, no head of a local state agency may react really autonomously ... Each participant both regulates and is regulated,' argues Thoenig (in 'Local Government Institutions,' p. 91). Machin's point is most strongly supported, however, when he refers to mayors of large towns who are also influential members of the (former) government majority. Historically, mayors close to the government of the day have controlled appointments to prefectures and field services. 'Advance consultation with pro-government deputies [and mayor/deputies] would appear to be the rule rather than the exception even today.' (Machin, 'Traditional Patterns of French Local Government,' in Lagroye and Wright, op. cit., p. 35.)
31. Pierre Birnbaum, 'Office Holders in the Local Politics of the French Fifth Republic,' in Lagroye and Wright, op. cit., p. 115.
32. Kesselman, *Ambiguous Consensus*, p. 129.
33. Becquart-Leclercq, *Paradoxes* ..., pp. 117–207.
34. Kesselman, *Ambiguous Consensus*, pp. 56–7. This is not to argue that one or several interests may not dominate the politics of a particular commune. Internal cohesiveness is generally characteristic of local government in Europe. See Linda Dolive, *Electoral Politics at the Local Level in the German Federal Republic* (Gainsville: University Presses of Florida, 1976), pp. 86–7; and A.J. Heidenheimer, H. Heclo and J. Adams, *Comparative Public Policy* (New York: St. Martin's Press, 1976), pp. 114–15. Heidenheimer *et al.* argue that, in dealing with local interest groups and in imposing public policy choices, European cities are stronger than those of the United States, despite (but in some cases, because of) the stronger national supervision of local affairs.
35. Webman, op. cit., p. 144.
36. Octave Gélinier, 'Vers de nouveaux concepts pour organiser l'administration,' in Peyrefitte *et al.*, *Décentraliser les responsabilités* (Paris: La Documentation Française, 1976), pp. 46–9.
37. Indeed, Webman's 'marble cake' model for urban redevelopment in Lyon is borrowed from Morton Grodzins, *The American Political System: A View of Government in the United States* (Chicago, 1966).
38. Louis Bériot, *36,000 maires en procès* (Paris: J-C. Lattes, 1977), pp. 8–9.
39. Ibid., p. 49.
40. Machin, 'Center and Periphery.'
41. For a summary of the provisions of the legislation passed in 1982 and 1983, see *Les Élections municipales de mars, 1983* (Paris: Supplément aux

dossiers du Monde, 1983), pp. 4–15; Mény, 'Decentralisation in Socialist France,' and Mark Kesselman, 'The Tranquil Revolution at Clochemerle: Socialist Decentralization in France,' in Philip Cerny and Martin A. Schain, eds, *Socialism: The State and Public Policy in France* (London: Frances Pinter, 1984). It would appear that in a number of ways the legislation 'rewards' local governments that have been most active in developing elements of autonomy in the past and tends to encourage such action in the future. Thus, Irene Wilson argues that local control over land use appears to be limited to the relatively few towns that have been or will be able to develop urban plans (POS). See Irene Wilson, 'Decentralizing or Recentralizing the State? Urban Planning and Center–Periphery Relations,' in Cerny and Schain, *Socialism: The State and Public Policy in France*.

42. Mény, 'Decentralisation in Socialist France,' p. 70.
43. Gary Meyers, 'After Jacobinism?: Center–Periphery Relations in Socialist France,' a paper delivered at the Annual Meeting of the American Political Science Association, Chicago, Ill., September 2, 1984, p. 4.
44. Gélinier, op. cit., pp. 48–50.
45. Meyers, op. cit., p. 35.
46. In fact, one criticism of the pre-1982 system of center–periphery relations was that it was 'a general system of irresponsibility,' in which no one actor was responsible for any decision that was made. One objective of the new legislation was to establish a clear division of functions among levels of government, an objective that does not appear to have been fulfilled, 'not that this is either possible or desirable in an age of highly complex government.' See François Dupuy and Jean-Claude Thoenig, 'La Loi du 2 mars 1982 sur la décentralisation. De l'analyse des textes à l'observation des premiers pas,' *Revue Française de Science Politique*, **33**, No. 6, December, 1983, pp. 964–5; and Douglas Ashford, 'The Socialist Reorganization of French Local Government — Another Jacobin Reform?' *Environment and Planning C: Government and Policy*, **1**, 1983, pp. 38–9.
47. Gremion and Worms, 'La Concertation régionale: innovation ou tradition?' in Institute d'Études Politiques de Grenoble, *Aménagement du territoire et développement régionale* (Paris: La Documentation Française, 1968), p. 59; Jeanne Becquart-Leclercq, *Paradoxes*, p. 205.
48. Jack Hayward, *The One and Indivisible French Republic* (New York: W.W. Norton, 1973), p. 32. Also, see Jean Houticq, 'L'Administration et la vie locale' (mimeographed course notes, Institut d'Études Politiques de Paris, 1963–4), p. 363, cited by Kesselman, *Ambiguous Concensus*, p. 145. Charles Riog notes that French local government is characterized less by centralization than by the maintenance of the status quo by complicity between central and local authorities, a point supported by J-C. Thoenig. (Riog, op. cit.: Thoenig, 'Local Government Institutions,' p. 93.)
49. Crozier and Friedberg, op. cit., p. 223; Hayward, op. cit., p. 35.
50. Thoenig, 'Local Government Institutions.' However, it is clear that political parties have been important in performing functions other

than those of setting priorities and linking the center to the periphery for coordination and influence. For example, party links with the governing majority have been important in establishing local influence over appointments (see n. 30). Also, local power has been important as a building block for national parties, and changing relations among national parties have been reflected in local politics. See Chapter 2.

51. Kesselman, 'The Tranquil Revolution,' p. 30.
52. Meyers, op. cit., pp. 31–2.
53. Kesselman, 'The Tranquil Revolution,' p. 30.
54. Becquart-Leclercq, 'Relational Power,' p. 15.
55. The most important published studies are Jean-Pierre Hoss, *Communes en banlieue: Argenteuil et Bézons* (Paris: Armand-Colin, 1969); Jerome Milch, 'Influence as Power: French Local Government Reconsidered,' *British Journal of Political Science*, **4**, 1974, pp. 139–62; Paul Thibault, 'Le Communisme municipal,' *Esprit*, October, 1967; Jean-Claude Ducros, 'Politique et finances locales,' *Analyses et Prévisions* II (1966): and Denis Lacorne, *Les Notables rouges: la construction municipale de l'union de la gauche (1971–77)* (Paris: Presses de la FNSP, 1981); and Pronier, op. cit. Milch and Lacorne make an attempt to integrate the Communist experience into more general considerations of French local politics and center–periphery relations, as does Sidney Tarrow, *Between Center and Periphery: Grass Roots Politicians in Italy and France* (New Haven: Yale University Press, 1977).
56. Pronier, op. cit., p. 12.
57. Crozier and Thoenig, op. cit., p. 22.
58. Lavau, op. cit.; Crozier and Friedberg, op. cit., p. 223; Becquart-Leclercq, *Paradoxes*, pp. 205–6; Kesselman, *Ambiguous Consensus*, p. 49.
59. Ronald Tiersky, *French Communism 1920–1972* (New York: Columbia University Press, 1977), p. 350.
60. Ibid. Also see Philip Williams, *Crisis and Compromise* (London: Longmans Green, 1964), p. 301.
61. The best study of the origins of Communist local government is an unpublished thesis by François Platone, 'L'Implantation municipale du parti communiste français dans la Seine et sa conception de l'administration communale' (mémoire, Diplôme supérieur d'études et de recherche politique, Paris, FNSP, 1967).
62. Ibid., *passim* and Tiersky, op. cit., p. 356.
63. Georges Lavau, in the 1981 study cited above, notes the dearth of scholarly work on the practice of Communist municipal government (p. 372) as does Pronier, in his 1983 study (p. 12). Most references to this subject draw on the same handful of studies cited in n. 55. Depth interviews were conducted with the mayor, several assistant mayors (*ajoints* — including at least one Socialist *ajoint* in each city), and other municipal officials, including the head of the municipal civil service (the *secrétaire-général*) wherever possible in the following cities:

    Cities where power changed hands in 1977: Athis-Mons; Houilles;

Sevran; Noisy-le-Grand; Antony; Villeneuve-Saint-Georges; Chelles; Poissy; Reims.

Cities governed by a Communist mayor before 1977: Arles; Sète; La Seyne; Venissieux; Vitry.

2 Electoral Support for Communist Local Governments: How Do They Gain and Maintain Electoral Power?

> The essential difference is that the Communists are more dissatisfied, more outraged by the State of Things, and consequently their protest vote is even more violent. They vote as far to the left as they can. If there were a party to the left of the Communist Party, they would vote for it. Furthermore, by voting Communist they are voting against their neighbors who vote Socialist and Socialist Radical. A Communist vote permits them to express their contempt of the inside *ils* and the outside *ils* at the same time. . . . However, it is only on this negative aspect of the Communist program that the members of the party find themselves in agreement.[1]

Communism in France has been generally understood from the perspective of protest and opposition. Supported by dissatisfied, deprived and alienated voters, the attractiveness of the party has been related more to its implacable anti-regime opposition than to its revolutionary vocation. In fact, so widespread has been the assumption of a link between Communist support and protest and alienation, that social scientists have frequently turned the relationship around and considered party membership and support as a measure in itself of the scope of alienated opposition in France.

However, the very nature of the support is the Achilles heel of the movement, since it is argued that support for the French Communist Party (PCF) should inevitably diminish as the conditions responsible for alienation recede. A party with little positive support, moreover, gains only as opposition, and is unlikely to gather support as a party with a serious chance of actually governing.

In recent years, this view of the PCF, and of support for the party has been effectively challenged.[2] However, support for the PCF at the one level of government where the party has held governing power for almost fifty years — the commune — has remained a neglected area of enquiry.[3]

This is particularly puzzling because, far from being exceptional, Communist government at the municipal level has been widespread and well established since the Second World War. In the provisional elections in 1945 almost 1,500 towns elected Communist mayors, including 46 of the 110 cities with more than 30,000 population. While many of these towns were lost in the Gaullist sweep of 1947, support for Communist local candidates and lists remained steady and strong during the Fourth and Fifth Republics, and the number of towns with Communist mayors grew steadily after 1947. Between 1959 and 1983, no Communist-led local government in a town with more than 30,000 population lost an election, and in each election the number of towns with Communist mayors increased. By 1965, Communist mayors governed more large towns than any other single party. Although this was no longer true after 1977, the Communist group has remained second only to the Socialists. (See Table 2.1.)

In the local elections of 1983, cities governed by Communists lost support for the first time since the establishment of the Fifth Republic, and the number of large towns governed by Communist mayors declined. This loss of support was not unexpected, since it confirmed the serious Communist losses in the presidential and legislative elections of 1981, as well as a reaction to the economic problems of the country, but it did indicate the limits of a long period of expansion of Communist local government. Nevertheless, it is clear that for many years a large number of voters have been willing to support Communists not simply as opposition, but as decision-makers and leaders of government.

We will argue here that the protest and opposition perspective, at least as it is generally presented, is an explanation that does not conform to the development or structure of support for Communist local government. The expansion and growth of electoral support was accomplished through a careful process of social and political coalition-building, while the decline in 1983 indicates some of the limits of that process. We shall argue

Table 2.1 *The number of towns with mayors of different parties during the Fifth Republic (cities with over 30,000 population)*

	1959	*1965*	*1971*	*1977*	*1983**
PC	25	34	45	72	57
PS (MRG)	41	33	40	83	63
Misc. left	17	14	9	8	0
Radical	6	6	4	2	
Centrist	12	13	26	9	40
Independent	15	13	11	13	
RI	8	8	12	15	
UNR-RPR	24	25	30	15	39
Diverse	10	12	15	3	21
Total	158	158	192	221	220

* These balances do not reflect simply the gains and losses of larger towns. They also reflect the results of population gains and losses. Thus ten towns that had 30,000 population in 1977 fell below that number in 1983, while nine towns grew beyond that level. These demographic changes decreased the number of larger Socialist-governed towns.

Sources: *Le Monde*, March 23, 1965, March 23, 1971, March 22, 1977; Gérard LeGall, 'Un recul du "bloc au pouvoir" moindre en 1983 qu'en 1977,' *Revue Politique et Parlementaire*, April 1983, p. 31.

that the expansion and decline reflect the strengths and weaknesses of established Communism in France, rather than the level of alienation in the country.

Explaining support for established Communism

Studies going back to the 1950s have emphasized the uniqueness of those who vote for the PCF, and have generally explained its electoral success in economic, sociological and psychological, rather than political, terms. Thus, the basis of Communist support is purported to be enduring poverty accentuated by large gaps between rich and poor.[4] Support is also nurtured by the isolation of some groups of workers from the rest of society. Therefore, support may be fixed in time to a transitional period of rapid industrial development, or fixed in social space (for railway workers, for example) or geographic space (for miners).[5]

The cumulative effect of these conditions, it has been argued, tends to foster working-class rootlessness and alienation, which forms the seedbed within which Communist support is established and grows. In this sense, Communism is 'the religion of the rootless' and support is the protest of the alienated.[6]

While work of Lipset and Kornhauser focuses on the conditions that form the context within which working-class alienation develops and is expressed, other studies deal directly with the nature of the alienation itself. What emerges is a pattern of strong, negative opposition. The Communist voter above all is opposed to 'the abstractions he feels are holding him back.' Support for the Communist Party has little to do with any positive agreement with the positions of the party, its programs and personnel; rather, it is simply the strongest expression of opposition to the existing system. Between the party and its supporters there is no shared perspective that goes beyond opposition and hostility towards the established political, social and economic order.

> It will have been noted by now that the one thing lacking in the reality world of the protest voter is some encompassing intellectual abstraction he is really and enthusiastically for: one consistent with the feelings he shares with so many others and with his most satisfying personal experiences; one that he and others can communicate and can rally around; one that rings as true for him today as the great political slogans of the eighteenth century did in their time.[7]

Given the sources of Communist strength, and the almost pure opposition that unites Communist support, the primary role of the party must be to maximize the political expression of discontent. In the short run this increases support: 'The social, economic and political issues remain, and with them, the impressive scope of Communist power to act as a disintegrating and corrupting element within our society.'[8] In the long run, however, modernization will eliminate the seedbed of protest support, and electoral support for the Communist Party will inevitably decline.

> If one admits that the true social revolution is taking place now through modernization, Communism seems fated in the West either to disappear or to remain only as an instrument of Soviet imperialism.[9]

Thus, the short-run stability of Communist support can be understood in terms of continuing sources of discontent and alienation. The logical consequence of this argument about the sources of Communist strength is to accept Communist electoral support as a measure, in itself, of the depth and breadth of systemic opposition, of widespread alienation and of weakness of the social fabric.

> Voting for a radical party is an aggressive form of alienation oriented against the existing socio-economic system, which aims at replacing the system with another. The percent of the radical vote is a good indicator of the extent of this kind of alienation.[10]

Other studies, however, offer a political explanation for the durability of Communist support that goes beyond alienation and that is related to the ability of the party to develop an effective organization. If Communist electoral support emerges from alienation, it is perpetuated through an isolating political subculture. Within the working-class core, the PCF has built political and electoral support on a counter-community structure.

> Stable Communist strength, that is, little fluctuation up or down, is associated with the older industrial areas in which the party has been strong since the Russian revolution . . . In such regions, the Communists have created an elaborate network of party-linked voluntary associations and leisure activities, so that, as in parts of France and Italy, one almost has a functioning subculture unaffected by political events . . . When the party is strong, it endeavors . . . to isolate its base from serious influence by non-Communist sources.[11]

Where they actually govern, they are in a stronger position, of course, to build a solid, oppositional counter-community.

> As the actual governors of a community, capable of producing political outputs more visibly than elsewhere, the Communists are able to serve this role in three ways: by answering the bread-and-butter interests of their clientele . . . , by making full use of a privileged channel of political communication, and by creating a network of solid Party bastions for use in both offensive and defensive strategy, depending on the exigencies of the moment. In other words, Communist local governments are important supports of the generalized roles of the tribune and countercommunity . . .[12]

Atomized, alienated, aggressive and even organized support, however, is quite different from support for the party as such, it is argued. Support for the party as opposition may be considerable, and even organizable, but this in no way presumes support for Communist Party power. The party voter 'measures his own satisfactions of life, not on Communist Party standards, but on middle class, bourgeois standards.'[13]

Thus the opposition–protest orientation of Communist support would appear to lock the party into a role of permanent opposition, since there always exists the danger of voters moving further to the left (or to the protest right for that matter). This analysis also implies that the Communist base is either highly politically unstable, or, alternately, subject to the influence of totalitarian controls.

Clearly, there are problems with this view of Communist electoral support as protest. Even if we accept the Communist Party as the party of the alienated and the politically disinherited, Georges Lavau has presented an impressive case that by effectively disengaging itself from revolutionary activity, and by committing itself to the electoral game, the PCF has provided an integrating bridge between the alienated and the Republic.[14] While this view has not gone unchallenged, Lavau presents extensive survey data to demonstrate that large numbers of voters — those who have voted Communist and those who have not — have *perceived* the Communists as 'tribunes' for the well-being of the dispossessed, rather than simply regime opponents.[15]

There is also evidence that the protest voter image of the PCF supporter has, at the very least, been exaggerated. For example, it is not at all clear that the Communists draw their support from the most impoverished groups. In various surveys taken during the Fifth Republic, the poorest categories gave more support to almost every major party over the PCF.[16] Nor was the income structure of PCF voters much different from that of any major party during the Fifth Republic; in fact, every major party drew a larger percentage than the Communists of its electorate from the lowest income groups.[17] With about half its votes coming from blue-collar workers, the PCF is certainly more dependent upon the working class than any other party. However, only about a third of blue-collar workers voted Communist in 1967, 1968, 1973 and 1978 (up from about a fifth in 1962) and fewer than a quarter voted Communist in the first round of the 1981 legislative elections. Moreover, it is important to remember that almost as many workers appear to have voted Gaullist in 1967 and 1968; the parties of the right lost working-class votes after 1973, but apparently to the Socialists. Finally, the unskilled, assembly-line workers were less likely than the skilled workers to vote for the PCF.[18] Thus, while alienation may be nurtured in an environment of relative deprivation, the Communist Party does not appear to have either an exclusive or a dominant claim on either the deprived or the working class.

Moreover, the claim that Communist Party supporters are alienated protest voters has to be analyzed in the context of French political culture. Statements describing a conflict society, or proposing that there is great injustice in France regularly receive a high level of agreement across party lines and class lines. Fifty-six percent of PCF respondents in 1968 agreed that 'class conflict is a reality:' but so did 50 percent of the Socialists and 40 percent of the Gaullists.[19] Also in 1968, fully two-thirds of the respondents agreed that increased wealth was being inequitably distributed, with little difference in the breakdown by party or class.[20] One analysis of mass orientations towards politics concluded that by the last months of the Fourth Republic, there was 'a tendency towards a national consensus against the parties and parliament.'[21]

Attitudes of alienation and opposition to various aspects of the political system have been quite common in France, and it is not clear that Communist supporters are different in this respect. PCF supporters do think of themselves, and are thought of by others as 'a useful force of opposition' and articulators of discontent.[22] However, Sidney Tarrow found that, in the early 1970s, political involvement among working-class respondents tended both to increase commitment to the left and decrease hostility to political leaders; among the working-class respondents, those most hostile to political leaders were least likely to be involved in politics and likely to support parties of the right.[23]

What has distinguished PCF supporters from those of other parties is not so much the negative bond of mere protest, but a much stronger bond of commitment. The response of Communist voters to questions concerning international events and the working-class condition has been strikingly different from that of other voters, and generally consistent with the party world view. PCF voters have also shown the strongest consistent loyalty to their party from election to election, and before 1982 were consistently favorable to participation of the party in responsible governmental positions.[24] In fact, if we take the attitudes and electoral behavior of Communist supporters as our guide, there seems to be more evidence of strong, widespread commitment to the PCF than to any other party. Whatever anger, protest or commitment attracts supporters to the party, the negative bond of protest seems to be an insufficient explanation for the stability and the growth of the Communist constituency until 1981.

Moreover, at least two studies of departments undergoing rapid industrial development show no consistent relationship between transitional economic development and changes in Communist support. The dislocations of development have increased PCF support under some circumstances, but have also increased support for the right under other conditions.[25]

Thus, analyses of voter attitudes and voting patterns bring into question the link between alienated protest and electoral support for the PCF. Nevertheless, it would be useful to pursue this analysis at the level where Communists have actually governed and held power, where the ability of the Communists to organize, isolate and perpetuate a counter-community has acquired mythical dimensions.[26]

The expansion and growth of electoral support at the local level

An analysis of voting patterns at the local level presents a complex picture that challenges both the link between protest voting and Communist support, as well as many of the prevailing assumptions about the ability of the PCF to organize politically and to perpetuate a counter-community. The establishment and expansion of Communist governments at the local level has always been conditional, and has been related more to their will and ability to operate within the political system, than to their desire to challenge the system directly. Until 1983, the electoral support for Communist local governments increased most during those periods when the party has either aspired to gain national governing power (1935 and 1977), or has actually held positions in the national government (1945–46). The greatest declines in support for Communists at the local level have occurred when the party has been most militantly revolutionary and has most openly challenged the regime.

The first breakthrough for the PCF in local elections was in 1935, when it doubled the number of cities under its control, from 150 to 297.[27] Ten years later, the second breakthrough occurred at a time when Communists held ministerial positions for the first time, and when the party was part of the governing coalition. The vote for Communist lists in local elections reached an all-time high in 1945 (5.5 million votes) and the number of towns with Communist mayors increased to almost 1,500.[28]

Local electoral support generally declined after the breakdown of the tripartite coalition in the spring of 1947 and local electoral success (i.e. actually winning elections) diminished rapidly. By 1965, the number of Communist local councilors and the number of towns with Communist mayors declined to about half the 1945 level.[29] As momentum increased in negotiations within the left on a common program, however, both electoral support and success increased. By 1977, the total number of towns with Communist mayors rose to about the same level as it had been in 1945.[30] Almost ten million people lived in towns with Communist mayors.

The general pattern of electoral success and failure until

1983 provides evidence that when the commitment of the PCF to govern was strong and clear, support and success increased, and declined when this commitment was ambiguous. In 1983, for the first time since the period of the liberation, local elections took place with the left actually in power at the national level, and with Communists holding ministerial positions. Once again voters were offered the possibility of voting their judgment of the Communists (and the Socialists) as national as well as local decision-makers and the judgment was 'globally negative.' For the first time during the Fifth Republic, the Communists suffered important losses in the larger towns (over 30,000 population). Electoral support declined by about 7 percent, and sixteen of the seventy-two towns with Communist mayors were lost to the right.[31] Communist-led lists lost votes in all but one of the towns controlled by the party. During the following year the Communists lost six more by-elections, held because of voting irregularities in March.

Although the scope and pattern of their losses were comparable to those of the Socialists, and less serious than those sustained by the right in 1977, they were quite serious from the point of view of the party organization. In areas in which the number of Communist-led governments had recently expanded, and where their defeats were concentratd, decline in electoral support was marginal. However, in areas where they had been in control the longest — the 'bastions' — decline was most pronounced, although there were few actual defeats of incumbent governments. (See below, pp. 43–6.)

If past patterns indicated a willingness by increasing numbers of voters to support Communists aspiring to attain national governing power, the 1983 local election results demonstrated a clear reaction to the way that power had been used. While support for Communist local government has always been conditional, the results also reflected the growing number of complex conditions that have underpinned the expansion and growth of support for Communist local government during the Fifth Republic.

Expansion of support and coalition-building

Changes in the electoral fortunes of Communist local

governments cannot be attributed to changes in electoral support alone. Electoral success since 1925 has also been related to such factors as electoral laws and, most of all, to cooperation within the left. (Of course, cooperation has also been related to periods when the PCF has pursued an electoral strategy.) Cooperation has usually benefited all parties, either through withdrawal in favor of the best-placed list in the second round of local elections, or through formation of combined 'popular-front' lists. Such agreements have increased success by eliminating destructive competition, even where actual voter support has changed very little.

Although widespread local agreements have been generally limited to periods when there has been agreement among the national parties, there have been local agreements even during the worst periods of internecine warfare on the left. In 1925, for example, in two of the five towns that elected Communist mayors in the Paris region (Malakoff and Vitry), there were local united lists with the SFIO.[32] In 1947 and 1953, on the other hand, cooperation at the local level was rare, and the Communists suffered massive defeats.

In 1947, Communist-led lists were defeated in thirty-five of the forty-six larger towns that they had governed since 1946. Twelve of these were clearly lost in 'duels' with the RPF, but the remainder of the defeats were due to the breakup of popular-front alliances with the Socialists. In numerous cities, Socialist town councilors voted with the Gaullists for either a Gaullist or Socialist mayor.[33] In the Paris region, the PCF lost forty of the sixty towns it controlled in 1946. In twenty-five of these towns, the Socialists were in a position to 'arbitrate,' and in twenty-one they used their position to gain the mayor's office, although in no case were they the strongest party.[34]

By contrast, in 1959, in the first local elections under the Fifth Republic, there were united lists in almost 20 percent of the 411 cities with more than 9,000 population. There were also numerous mutual withdrawals in the second round of the elections, despite efforts by the national Socialist Party to keep the Communists isolated. As a result, there were important gains for both parties.[35]

The importance of the combined effects of the electoral law and electoral cooperation can be seen through an analysis of Communist victories in towns with over 30,000 population during the Fifth Republic. Of the seventy-two large towns governed by the Communists prior to the 1983 elections, only sixteen had been in their control after the 1947 Gaullist sweep. In each succeeding election the PCF was able to increase the number of larger towns under its control.

Increased electoral support was only marginally important for most of the initial victories in each election. The first large increase in the number of municipalities with Communist mayors occurred in 1959, and can be attributed more to the operation of the new election law, than to any massive shift of voters in favor of the Communists. The new law substituted a winner-take-all system (in municipalities with fewer than 120,000 people) for the previous system of proportional representation. Three of the ten victories in 1959 were achieved by a plurality in the second round; these municipalities probably would have gone to a non-Communist coalition under the old system. In three others, the Communists owed their victory to the organization of popular front lists (Noisy-le-Sec, Patin and Choissy-le-Roi).[36] In only three of the remaining five was there a decisive Communist electoral victory with a majority on the first round. The mean vote in the first round for the Communist-led lists was only 44.8 percent, three points higher than in the previous election.

Similarly, of the eight large municipalities that elected Communist mayors in 1965, four were won with joint lists, and one other with withdrawal of the Socialist list in the second round. In two of the remaining three, the Communist-led won a plurality in both rounds. In the last, le Havre, the Communist list, led by a former mayor, gained a majority in the second round. However, because the Communists did not have a majority in the first round, they gained control of the city council only because the election rules for cities with more than 120,000 population were changed in 1965 from proportional representation to winner-take-all in the second round.

By 1971, the movement towards unity on the left had begun in earnest, and five of the six new municipalities that elected Communist mayors did so with Communist-Socialist lists. The 1977 municipal elections marked an unprecedented victory for the united left in general, and the Communists in particular. The number of Communist-governed municipalities increased by twenty-two. Twenty of these lists were union of the left coalitions with the Socialists. In the remaining two, La Ciotat and Noisy-le-Grand, the Socialist Party split, enabling the United Left list to win a first-round victory, and in the second, the Socialists withdrew their list for the second round. However, in no case can the PCF victory be attributed to an upsurge in support for the Communist Party.[38]

Therefore, the electoral laws since 1959, which have generally favored party coalitions and cooperation, combined with increasing cooperation among the parties of the left, have provided a framework within which the Communists have been able to maneuver either to win all of the municipal council seats with a plurality of votes, or (increasingly) to expand their local influence through the development and the enforcement of left-unity. The point is that increased voter support has been of only marginal importance for most of the initial victories, and that the alteration of the political environment has been of far greater importance — at least for the initial victory.

Aside from the election laws, the second important change in the political environment has been the restructuring of the Socialist Party at the local level. Despite the national strategy to which the PS was committed after 1972, thirty of the forty-six municipalities with Socialist mayors before the 1977 elections were governed either by non-Communist-left or 'Third Force' coalitions.[39] This reflected the reality of the Socialist Party at the grass roots when the feeling was still strong that the strength of the party lay in its ability to form either coalitions of the center or the left, depending on the local situation, and that it could maximize its strength nationally through local flexibility. In addition, many of the party's important local notables had built their careers on fighting and defeating the Communists at the local level.[40]

The PS was changing, however, particularly in the larger cities. With considerable caution, the new party leadership had begun to break up some of the old Third Force alliances at the local level even before the 1971 local elections.

> In 1965, and even more in 1971, a 'new' Third Force tactic was not likely to be successful, particularly not in a large city for the simple reason that its acceptance almost always implied the disruption of the local Socialist section and favored the

> establishment of rival Socialist factions thus splitting the Socialist electorate.[41]

Frequently, Socialist leaders at the department level intervened directly to prevent the formation of Third Force coalitions, and at times PS and PCF section leaders at the local level intervened as well. Where higher party intervention at the local level was resisted, advocates of Third Force strategy were sometimes either dismissed from the party, or resigned in anticipation of dismissal. Thus, after 1965, there was a gradual 'nationalization' of Socialist politics that permitted an expansion of Communist influence at the local level.[42]

In anticipation of the 1977 municipal elections, the Communists now demanded that the PS intensify its efforts to restructure the party at the local level. In the short run this would be a test of viability of the united-left strategy; in the long run it would serve to neutralize the most anti-Communist elements within the PS. As a result, an agreement was reached at the national level on June 28, 1976 that required the departmental and local organizations of both parties to negotiate united lists for the first round of the elections.[43]

For the Communists, there were several important results of the general success of this operation. The united-left coalitions enabled both parties to expand their presence at the local level, and for both the gamble was fully justified by the results. Despite the turmoil that accompanied the restructuring in numerous cases, party loyalty remained generally strong, and united-left lists were victorious in fifty-seven new municipalities: twenty-two where the PCF headed the list and thirty-five where the PS headed the list. Perhaps more important, the Communists lost none of the municipalities they held before the elections, while the Socialists lost only six (one to the Communists). Thus, the viability of the coalition was demonstrated. Also, the PCF entered the governing councils of twenty-five cities that were formerly governed by non-Communist-left or Third Force coalitions (the PS entered the councils of nine PCF-governed cities from which they had been previously excluded). This breakthrough, and the forced resignation or dismissal of five Socialist mayors, was of long-term importance for the Communists, since the strategy of cooperation set into motion a process that greatly expanded the presence of the party.[44]

This process contradicts the widely-held belief that the expansion of Communist government at the local level was '... above all due to an anti-Gaullist reflex among a large number of voters.'[45] During the Fifth Republic, many of the Communist victories were at the expense of Socialist or centrist Third Force coalitions. Although a number of more recent victories were 'duels' between left and right coalitions, the record does not support the contention that Communist expansion was basically a reactive and negative reflex. The expansion of Communist local government (and therefore the limit to that expansion) can be attributed, in large measure, to the slow disintegration of Third Force coalitions at the local level under the pressure of left unity. Of course, this too can be seen as a reflex against the right, but by the parties, not the voters. This process also greatly altered the social environment within which the Communists held local power.[46]

The changing social environment

Cities in which PCF mayors have held power since 1947 are mostly the working-class suburbs of Paris; only two are outside the Paris region. Municipalities that have elected Communist-led lists since 1953, however, have been increasingly less working class and are in other parts of the country. In 1968, a third of the larger towns governed by Communists had working-class majorities, but by 1978, only 13 percent were predominantly working class. In 1968, fewer than a quarter of the Communist-governed towns were outside the Paris region, but by 1978, 40 percent were in the provinces. (See Table 2.2.)

Three kinds of changes have contributed to this altered environment. The most important is the development of coalition politics within the left, which made possible a large number of victories of Communist-led lists during the Fifth Republic. Only three of the forty-two larger towns won by the Communists after local coalition-building began (in 1965) had majority working-class populations. Second, the social structure of the population has been changing since the Second World War, even in the older bastions. Among the sixteen larger towns governed by Communists since 1947 (or

Table 2.2 *The distribution of Communist-governed towns in 1968 and 1978 by location and by working-class population (percentage of towns over 30,000 population)*

	1968 (N = 34)			*1978 (N = 72)*		
	*High working class** %	*Low working class** %	*Total 1968* %	*High working class** %	*Low working class** %	*Total 1978* %
Paris region	24	52	76	5	54	59
Provinces	9	14	23	8	32	40
Total	33	66	100	13	86	100

* Cities with over 30,000 population and more than 50 percent blue-collar workers.

Sources: Population figures are taken from *Le Recensement de la population, 1968, 1975* (Paris INSEE, 1970 and 1978).

before), almost 60 percent had working-class majorities in 1968, but this diminished to 25 percent by 1975. Finally, an increasing percentage of this working-class population in the older bastions was composed of immigrant workers who could not vote, thus diluting working-class electoral strength even more.[47]

By 1983, as a result of these changes, the network of Communist-governed municipalities was somewhat more working class than towns governed by other parties, but not strikingly different from those governed by the Socialists (See Table 2.3.) Indeed, the class profile of Communist-governed towns (and those governed by the left in general) was far more typical of larger cities in France than the class profile of cities governed by the right. If the 'typical' Communist town has been understood as a working-class suburb of Paris, the 'typical' town that elected a new Communist mayor during the Fifth Republic was a provincial town with a working-class minority.

Table 2.3 *Distribution of towns governed by different parties — 1983 (before the elections) by working-class concentration (cities with over 30,000 population)*

% Working class		*PC*	*PS/MRG*	*MOD*	*Gaullist*	*Local*	*Total*
0–30	Number	4	12	9	6	3	34
	Percent	5.4%	14%	23.7%	60%	30%	15.6%
31–50	Number	60	62	29	4	7	162
	Percent	81%	72.9%	76.3%	40%	70%	74.7%
50%+	Number	10	11	0	0	0	21
	Percent	13.5%	12.9%	0	0	0	9.7%
Total	Number	74*	85	38	10	10	217
	Percent	100%	100%	100%	100%	100%	100%

* includes two towns where the population exceeded 30,000 by 1983.
Sources: population figures are taken from *Le Recensement de la population, 1975* (Paris: INSEE, 1978).

The growth and decline of Communist electoral support

Although increased support for the PCF has been less important than coalitions and changing support in accounting for initial Communist victories in most cases, once the Communists were in power support grew impressively until 1983. Eleven municipalities elected PCF-led councils in 1959. In the first round of the elections, the mean vote for these lists was 41.1 percent. In 1965, it increased to 58.4 percent, in 1971 it stayed about the same, and rose to 63.5 percent in 1977. Similarly, in 1965 nine large municipalities elected a Communist list for the first time with an average of 43.4 percent of the votes in the first round. This rose to 56.1 percent in 1971 and 60.2 percent in 1977.

In general, those towns that have been governed by Communists for the longest period of time voted for them in the highest proportions. (See Table 2.4.) The vast majority of the towns that were governed by Communists for twelve years or longer in 1977 gave them more than 60 percent of the vote.

Table 2.4 *Electoral support for Communist-governed towns in 1977 and 1983, by years in power (towns with over 30,000 population) (percentage in first round of local election).*

	Years in power in 1983						
	36	*30*	*24*	*18*	*12*	*6*	*Total*
1977	76%	70%	63%	60%	58%	48%	61%
1983	61	60	53	51	47	47	53
Mean loss	15	10	10	9	11	1	8
No. of towns	16	7	11	9	7	22	72

Sources: Le Monde, March 15, 1977; March 8, 1983.

Although this comfortable margin was sharply reduced in 1983, the relationship between level of electoral support and length of time in office was confirmed. Thus, if the changing political environment facilitated the *emergence* of Communist-led governments in a growing number of cities with more complex class structures, the experience of voters with these governments resulted in an *increase* of support in subsequent elections, at least until 1983.

The 1983 municipal elections altered the trends of the previous twenty-four years. For the first time during the Fifth Republic, recently-elected Communist municipalities failed to increase their proportion of the vote, and in the oldest bastions of Communist strength there was a heavy erosion of electoral support for the first time since the Second World War.

In the most competitive marginal towns (from an electoral point of view), those won in 1977, Communist-led lists lost less than one percent of their 1977 vote. Even in towns that were lost to the opposition, the loss was 3 percent. A large number of the defeats that were sustained can be attributed to a weakening of the political coalition between the Communists and the Socialists at the local level, and a comparative strengthening of the coalition of the right. In seven of the sixteen towns that were lost to the Communists, the parties of the left ran separate lists in the first round; three of these towns were lost in the first round to a more unified opposition. In the second round, at least three more were lost because of a weak transfer of votes from the Socialists (who had withdrawn) to the remaining Communist list.[48] Thus the election demonstrated the strength of the social coalition upon which the expansion of Communist local governments was based, while it also showed the fragility of the political coalition, and the degree to which the maintenance of Communist local government is based upon political agreement.

The 15 percent decline of electoral support in the oldest bastions was far more serious, and accentuated some differences between areas of established Communist strength and the more marginal areas, particularly at times when electoral trends were changing nationally. The last important decline of electoral support for the Communists at the local level was in 1947, a decline that we have attributed to a protest against the movement towards an oppositional position by the party nationally. Although the loss of votes nationally was substantial in 1947, it was only marginal in the bastions of the Paris region.[49] In 1983, the most substantial losses, and the highest rates of abstention were in the 'bastions.'[50]

Voting patterns during the Fifth Republic do not support the thesis that support for Communist local governments is simply a manifestation of negative protest against the central authority of governments of the right. Local support has been stable and has grown as these governments have become better established, and stable voting patterns are not usually characteristic of the protest voters.[51] Moreover, many of the same voters who have voted for Communist governments at the local level have voted for center-right candidates at the national level, behavior that would certainly contradict an interpretation of their local voting as a protest against the right. (See below.)

On the other hand, voting patterns reveal a pattern of protest directed against the Communists at particular moments: in 1947, in the marginal towns, against the shift of PCF policy in the Cold War; in 1983, in the bastions, against the policies of a government of the left in which the PCF shared responsibility. While willing to support Communist local governments when the party was in opposition, large numbers of voters in the bastions now cast their votes in reaction to their strong feelings about key national issues, experienced more acutely in the older industrial towns than in the newly-won towns. (See below, pp. 51–2.)

In the bastions, as in other towns, the electoral support for Communist lists has been far in excess of the number of working-class voters during the Fifth Republic, and the high levels of support have been due to the votes of white-collar workers. It appears from national surveys that while working-class voters remained most loyal to the left in 1983, particularly in towns governed by Communist or Socialist mayors, white-collar workers deserted the left in the highest proportions.[52] Therefore, by 1983, even the bastions were dependent on white-collar support, and vulnerable to white-collar concerns and disappointments. This protest vote, directed against the Communists, is clearly different, however, from a protest vote in favor of the Communists and against the right.

The maintenance of support: the 'breaking effect' and the isolated working-class community

Nevertheless, throughout the Fifth Republic electoral support for the Communist-governed municipalities has been strong and stable. However, it is certainly possible that this support can be explained more by working-class loyalties and by the effectiveness of local party organizations, than by the attractions of Communist local government.

Because of a combination of class solidarity and the pressure exerted by a large working-class community, we would expect to find disproportionately high levels of support for Communist candidates in cities with larger working-class populations — a phenomenon referred to by Robert Lane as 'the breaking effect.'[53] Also, because the party organization is more solidly entrenched in the older bastions, particularly those with large working-class populations, we would expect to find consistency of electoral support in these towns.[54]

Support for Communist-led lists, however, has not been affected in any predictable way by working-class concentration. Support levels in 1977 and 1983 varied with length of time in office, regardless of working-class population. If, for example, we compare the cities where Communist governments were elected in 1947 or before with those where Communist mayors were first elected in 1977, we find that in the 1977 and 1983 elections the level of electoral support was highest where the concentration of working-class population was smallest for the 1947 group, indicating no breaking effect. (See Table 2.5.) However, the towns with the largest working-class populations suffered smaller losses of votes in 1983, indicating greater working-class loyalty, or the effectiveness of the local party machine.

Table 2.5 *Percentage of the vote won with Communist-led lists in 1977 and 1983 by working-class concentration (cities of over 30,000 population)*

Percent working class (1975)	*Elected 1947 or before*				*Elected 1977*			
	(N)	*% 1977*	*% 1983*	*Difference*	*(N)*	*% 1977*	*% 1983*	*Difference*
50–9%	(4)	73.8%	61.8%	−12.0%	(1)	50.3%	49.2%	−1.1%
40–9%	(9)	75.3%	58.6%	−16.5%	(9)	48.3%	51.0%	+2.7%
30–9%	(3)	83.2%	67.2%	−16.0%	(12)	47.3%	48.9%	+1.6%

Sources: *Le Monde*, March 15, 1977; March 8, 1983.

In the marginal towns captured in 1977, the breaking effect should be more important, since the party machine did not have time to take root in 1977. However, there was very little variation in support levels in 1977 and 1983. In fact, those with the largest working-class populations lost votes relative to 1977, while the others actually gained votes. (See Table 2.5.)

It is also possible that Communist electoral stability can be explained by the successful work of local parties in creating an isolating political culture from a more dynamic and complex social base. One way to explore this hypothesis is to compare the consistency of local and national election results in those towns where the party organization can be presumed to be strongest. If the link between effective party domination and electoral success is strong, party influence should be as strong in national as in local elections.

However, there is considerable evidence that the party machine is less effective than its reputation. In the 1973 National Assembly elections, when the Communists generally regained their 1967 level of electoral support, the PCF reported that 58 percent of the towns governed by Communists (with greater than 10,000 population) lost votes compared with 1967. Among the 42 percent that gained votes over 1967, the gains were greatest in the *newer*, less-established municipalities. Thus, the party argued that its organizational strength in more-established towns did not seem to aid their national electoral success. Indeed, the party committee argued that the less-established municipalities were more successful because of '... the impact of renovation and reinforcement of the party and the working class.'[55]

Similarly, in 1978 the PCF vote remained stable nationally, and there were gains in forty-four departments, compared with 1973. However, in the Paris region there was a general decline in the vote for the Communists '... including the two strong bastions of the Seine-Saint-Denis, where the PCF progressed only in the ninth circumscription, and in the Val-de-Marne, where it generally declined, often seriously.'[56]

If we compare the vote for the Communist-led lists in the bastions of the Paris region in the first round of the 1977 local elections with both the first rounds of the legislative elections a year later and the presidential election four years later, once again we find that political implantation is not easily transformed into political effectiveness. (See Table 2.6.) With a mean vote of 75 percent, Communist-led lists mobilized more than 60 percent of the vote in 1977 in all but one of the twenty-one bastions. In the legislative elections a year later, electoral support for Communist candidates was much less impressive. In many of the bastions, Communist candidates confronted opponents from the left, as well as the right. The mean PCF vote was 51.3 percent, and in none of these towns did the Communist candidate receive more than 60 percent of the vote. In a third of the bastions the candidate attracted less than half the vote. In the second round, when there was no longer any opposition from the left, the mean vote rose to 68 percent, seven points below the 1977 showing. This gap between local and national support confirms the findings of Dupoirier and Grunberg for the 1965–71 period.[57]

In the presidential election of 1981, the First Secretary of the PCF was unable to command a majority in any of the bastions in the first round. Indeed, he received a mean of only 36

Table 2.6 *Distribution of votes for the PCF in the 21 bastions* in the Paris Region in 1977, 1978, 1981 and 1983 (number of towns in each category — 1st round of each election, percentage of expressed votes)*

	1977 (munic.)	*1978 (legis.)*	*1981 (pres.)*	*1983 (munic.)*
70% +	16			4
60–9%	4	1		10
50–9%	1	13		7
40–9%		5	4	
30–9%		2	16	
20–9%			1	
Total	21	21	21	21
Mean vote	75.3%	51.3%	35.6%	67.7%

* Cities governed by Communist mayors before the Fifth Republic — cities over 30,000 population.

Sources: *Le Monde*, March 15, 1977; March 15, 1978; March 8, 1983. *Le Monde*, L'Élection presidentielle 26 avril–10 mai, 1981 (*Supplèment aux dossiers et documents du Monde*, mai, 1981), pp. 153–190.

percent of the vote in these towns (with little deviation from this mean). Despite the setbacks in the 1983 elections in the bastions, the results confirm that local support cannot be transferred easily. The mean of 67.7 percent is far below the 1977 level, but far above the support levels of 1981 and 1978.

Therefore, if we use electoral support for Communist candidates as a rough index of party effectiveness, we must conclude that the influence and the ability of the party to mobilize electoral support is qualified and limited. Able to mobilize impressive though limited support in local elections, where candidates may be known, are close to home and have developed a record in governing, the party is far less effective in mobilizing support for Communist candidates in the broader electoral arenas. The emphasis on both the breaking effect and organizational control as explanations for the maintenance of local support appears to be exaggerated, since electoral support mobilized in this way should be transferable to

Table 2.7 *Voters' orientations toward local governments*

	Party preference				
	PCF	*Non-Comm. left*	*Centrist*	*RI*	*UDR*
1. Do you feel it is a good thing or a bad thing that a mayor has a political tendency? *%age who feel it is good:*	52%	39%	26%	29%	31%
2. Mayors do not have enough freedom to direct their communes. *%age who disagree:*	32%	20%	24%	27%	25%
3. It is better that communes do not have budgets that are too large because they do not know how to use them. *%age who agreed:*	17%	19%	17%	23%	24%

Sources: *Sondages* 1971, nos 1 and 2, pp. 79 and 82.

different kinds of elections. Voters who give overwhelming support to Communist local candidates are quite capable of withdrawing that support from other candidates. In fact, local Communist governments appear to attract support in their own right.

Conditional and ideological support

There is some limited evidence that what has attracted voters to support local Communist governments is both positive and somewhat different from what has attracted voters to other alternatives. Communist voters are more politicized in the sense that they tend to link local and national party politics, and that they think that this linkage is a good thing. On the other hand, they profess relatively strong faith in the liberty of action of local government as more positive and more innovative than do voters for other parties. (See Table 2.7.)

Thus, one survey indicated that the highest priority among those voting Communist on the local level is the development of public services. While this was a priority for those voting for other left parties (mostly Socialist), in contrast to those voting for the right, far more Communist voters also ranked greater citizen participation as a priority in contrast to those voting for other parties. In addition, fewer Communist supporters regarded the defense of local interests as a priority compared with other voters. (See Table 2.8.) These priorities are reflected in the orientations of the Communist mayors who tend to justify their actions in terms of 'the public interest' far more than mayors of other parties, and are deeply involved in the administrative complexities of developing local projects, according to Sydney Tarrow.[58]

Table 2.8 *Of the following municipal functions, which do you regard as the most important?*

	Traditionalist		*Modernist*		*Participationist*	
	Satisfactory administration of local services	*Champions local interests vis-à-vis the central government*	*Develops public services*	*Prepares for further development*	*Secures greater participation by inhabitants*	*Represents political attitudes*
Total	49%	40%	45%	38%	21%	1%
Party Pref:						
PCF	43	36	49	33	30	3
Non-Comm. left	45	39	49	41	22	3
Center	56	51	39	27	25	
Gaullist	53	38	40	40	23	

Sources: Derived from Jack Hayward and Vincent Wright, 'The 37708 Microcosms of an Indivisible Republic: The French Local Elections of March, 1971,' *Parliamentary Affairs*, Autumn 1971, p. 234.

Until 1981, these orientations probably helped to maintain and increase the levels of support for Communist local government. However, after 1981, the opposite was probably true. The orientation towards local–national party linkage facilitated a left protest vote that was most evident where support had been most stable and durable. About 4 of the 14 percent of the electorate that voted for Mitterrand in the second round of the 1981 presidential election, but voted for the right in 1983, changed their vote for 'local reasons,' and most of these voted in towns dominated by the right. Most of the remaining 10 percent, those concerned with national issues, voted in towns governed by the left.[59]

Almost 40 percent of those who changed their vote to the right were concerned about unemployment (which was also the dominant concern for 64 percent of those who continued to vote for the left and 45 percent of the general electorate). Two national issues, however, concerned many more of these who switched to the right than other voters: security and immigrants, issues that most easily link local politics to national responsibility.[60]

If support for Communist local government has been more than merely the rejection of the right, rejection of Communist local government is linked to rejection of the policies of a national government with which the Communists have been associated. Although 52 percent of those who responded (to a SOFRES survey) in February 1983 were more confident of the left to run local government than of the right, 61 percent declared their desire 'to manifest their discontent with the left.'[61]

* * *

We have found that the more conventional, oppositional interpretation of support for Communist local government is helpful neither for understanding the development and maintenance of that support, nor for understanding the changes indicated by the results of the 1983 local elections. The view of electoral support as a manifestation of working-class alienation and party manipulation both overestimates the effectiveness of the party and ignores important elements with which support has been built.

Closer investigation reveals that even in areas of working-class strength, the party has not been able to mobilize a consistent, dependable constituency, and that electoral support for Communist-led local governments almost always exceeds support for Communists running for national office in the same towns. Increasingly, stable support has expanded to areas outside of the older core areas, but this support has also been conditional. The results of the 1983 elections confirm the stability of this support, but also confirm the conditions that make it possible, the most important of which is the ability of the Communists to attract multiclass support, which is related to continuing political cooperation within the left.

The oppositional interpretation of electoral support implies a level of unconditional ideological commitment by voters to the PCF that may never have existed. As Communist government expanded at the local level during the Fifth Republic, it was built on a complex set of conditions. Voters were asked to vote for Communist-led lists in order to achieve local change and reform and to manifest their support for the unity of the left, and voters from diverse backgrounds responded in growing numbers. The results of the 1983 elections serve to remind us that social and political bases for Communist local government have changed during the Fifth Republic. Political coalitions, built around programs, objectives and diverse party loyalties have modified, and perhaps replaced, the old ideological community. The party seems to have succeeded in building a different kind of electoral support, at once broader and more conditional.

In fact, it appears that in important ways the expectations of supporters of Communist government at the local level are related to what they have obtained. We have found considerable confirmation that both the policy choices and the processes through which these choices are made are different in cities governed by Communist mayors, and that these choices generally conform to the model of local government favored by those who support Communist local governments.

Notes

1. Laurence Wylie, *Village in the Vaucluse* (New York: Harper, 1964), p. 219.
2. In, for example, Georges Lavau, *A quoi sert le parti communiste français?* (Paris: Fayard, 1983). Lavau, however, presents a functional argument that 'the PCF legitimates the system, while constantly crying about its legitimacy . . .' by acting as a 'tribune' for the alienated while acting within the confines of the rules of the game. Thus, alienated opposition is channelled into the system in legitimate ways. See pp. 34–8. Also see Richard Hamilton, *Affluence and the French Worker in the Fourth Republic* (Princeton: Princeton University Press, 1967), Introduction and pp. 290–8.

3. Raymond Pronier, *Les Municipalités communistes* (Paris: Balland, 1983), p. 12. Pronier somewhat exaggerates. There are a few studies of Communist municipalities that will be referred to below. However, interest has certainly been peripheral. Although Elisabeth Dupoirier and Gerard Grunberg of CIVIPOF in Paris have collected extensive data on voting at the municipal level, there has been no important study of voting patterns in Communist municipalities. Pronier's study (475 pages) devotes little space to electoral support.
4. Seymour Martin Lipset, *Political Man* (New York: Anchor, 1963), pp. 45 and 125.
5. William Kornhauser, *The Politics of Mass Society* (New York: Free Press, 1959), p. 213 and Ch. 5, *passim*.
6. Ibid., p. 157.
7. Hadley Cantril and David Rodnick, *On Understanding the French Left* (Princeton: Institute for International Research, 1956), p. 151.
8. Mario Einaudi, 'Communism in Western Europe,' in Einaudi, Domenach and Garoschi, *Communism in Western Europe* (Hamden: Anchor Books, 1971), p. 51.
9. Pierre Fougeyrollas, 'France,' *Survey*, June 1962, p. 124.
10. Glaucio Soares and Robert L. Hablin, 'Socio-economic Variables and Voting for the Radical Left in Chile, 1952,' *The American Political Science Review*, December, 1967, p. 1,053.
11. Seymour Martin Lipset, 'The Changing Class Structure and Contemporary European Politics,' *Daedelus*, Winter 1964, p. 290. Also, see Hamilton, op. cit.
12. Ronald Tiersky, *French Communism 1920–1972* (New York: Columbia University Press, 1974), p. 352.
13. Cantril and Rodnick, op. cit., p. 151.
14. Lavau, op. cit. Also see his article, 'The PCF, the State and Revolution,' in Donald Blackmer and Sidney Tarrow, *Communism in Italy and France* (Princeton: Princeton University Press, 1975). Lavau's views have not gone uncontested. See the article by Annie Kriegel, 'The French Communist Party and the Fifth Republic,' in the same volume, as well as *Les Communistes* (Paris, Éditions du Seuil, 1970) pp. 238–47.
15. We should add that, perceptions aside, the PCF has not been in the lead of protest mobilization for some time. The most determined protests during the Fifth Republic have been organized by former Catholic trade unionists and peasant militants, as well as violently anti-Communist students. Lavau notes that in Stanley Hoffman's article, 'Protest in Modern France' (in Morton Kaplan, *The Revolution in World Politics*), the PCF is not mentioned a single time. Lavau, 'Le Parti communiste dans le système politique français,' in Frédéric Bon *et al.*, *Le Communisme en France* (Paris: Armand Colin, 1969), pp. 28–31, 39.
16. See *Sondages*, 1963, No. 2, p. 64. In the first round of the presidential elections in 1981, Georges Marchais, the candidate for the Communist Party, received a lower percentage of the vote than any other major candidate in two income categories — the lowest and the highest. See *Le Nouvel Observateur*, June 1, 1981, p. 40.
17. *Sondages*, 1966, No. 2. For additional comments, see Thomas Greene,

'The Electorate of Non-Ruling Communist Parties,' *Studies in Comparative Communism*, July–October, 1971, p. 82.

18. *Sondages*, 1967, No. 3, p. 55; 1968, No. 2, p. 102; 1973, No. 1, p. 21; 1978, No. 1, p. 22. *Le Nouvel Observateur*, July 4, 1981. In fact the proportion of working-class votes among the PCF electorate has declined slightly from 53 percent in 1973 to about 49 percent in 1981.
19. *Sondages*, 1968, No. 1, p. 45.
20. Ibid., p. 43.
21. Pierre Fougeyrollas, *La Conscience politique dans la France contemporaine* (Paris: Denoël, 1963), p. 185.
22. Lavau, 'Le Parti communiste . . .,' pp. 30–1.
23. Sidney Tarrow, 'Urban–Rural Cleavages and Political Involvement: The Case of France,' *American Political Science Review*, June 1971, p. 350.
24. Fougeyrollas, *La Conscience* . . ., Ch. 2, and Greene, op. cit., pp. 73–89.
25. Greene, op. cit., p. 101. Also see François Goguel, *Modernisation économique et comportement politique* (Paris: Armand Colin, 1969), pp. 81–7.
26. For example, see the volume by the journalist Jean Montaldo, *L'État Communiste* (Paris: Albin Michel, 1978), especially Chapters 4 and 5.
27. Daniel Brower, *The New Jacobins* (Ithaca: Cornell University Press, 1968), p. 86.
28. *L'Année Politique*, 1944–45 (Paris: Presses Universitaires de France, 1946), p. 491; *L'Année Politique*, 1947, p. 364.
29. *Le Monde*, April 23, 1971, p. 10.
30. For a listing of towns and their Communist mayors, see *Communes d'Aujourd'hui*, No. 10, 1977, p. 43.
31. See Gérard Le Gall, 'Un recul du "bloc au pouvoir" moindre en 1983 qu'en 1977,' *Revue Politique et Parlementaire*, April 1983.
32. François Platone, 'L'Implantation municipale du Parti communiste dans la Seine et sa conception de l'administration communale,' (unpublished memoire, DES, FNSP, Paris, 1967), p. 12.
33. Frédéric Bon and Jérôme Jaffré, 'Les Résultats des élections municipales de 1947,' FNSP, colloque des 4 et 5 décembre, 1981, pp. 14–20.
34. Platone, op. cit., p. 32.
35. *Le Monde*, March 19, 1959. Also see Roy Macridis and Bernard Brown, *The De Gaulle Republic* (Homewood: Dorsey Press, 1960), pp. 279–82.
36. *Le Monde*, March 19, 1959, p. 5.
37. *Le Monde*, March 16 and 23, 1965.
38. Indeed, Jean Charlot found that the victories for the left were probably due more to support for the Socialists. See Charlot, 'Avant l'empoignade du 2[e] tour,' *Le Point*, March 4, 1977.
39. See Jean Charlot, 'La Politisation des municipales,' *Projet*, February 1977, p. 139.
40. See Denis Lacorne in Blackmer and Tarrow, op. cit., pp. 335–9.
41. Ibid., p. 321.

42. The definitive book on the development of unity of the left at the local level is Denis Lacorne, *Les Notables rouges* (Paris: Presses de la FNSP, 1980). On the intervention of the national Socialist Party, see pp. 153–61.
43. Ibid., p. 162. Also see Jack Hayward and Vincent Wright, 'Governing from the Center, the 1977 French Local Elections,' *Government and Opposition*, Autumn 1977, pp. 40–1.
44. For the results of the elections, see *Le Monde*, March 15 and 22, 1977 and *Regards sur l'Actualité*, Ministry of the Interior, April 1977, pp. 58–64; report of Roger Fajardie of the PS, *Le Monde*, March 27–8, 1977.
45. *L'Année Politique*, 1965, p. 26.
46. See Lacorne, *Les Notables rouges*, p. 125.
47. Immigrants comprised 13.2 percent of the population of the bastions in 1968, and 16.4 percent in 1975. This percentage has certainly increased since 1975. In 1975 all Communist-governed cities had a mean immigrant population of 12 percent, higher than that of groups of cities governed by any other party. On the question of immigrant workers and local politics, see my article, 'Immigrants and Politics in France: Local Politics, Socialism and Race,' in John S. Ambler, ed., *France Under Socialist Leadership* (Philadelphia: Institute for the Study of Human Issues, forthcoming).
48. Jean-Luc Parodi, 'Dans la logique des élections intermédiares,' *Revue Politique et Parliamentaire*, April 1983, p. 64.
49. *L'Année Politique*, 1947, pp. 193–4.
50. Le Gall, op. cit., pp. 16–17.
51. On this question, see Angus Campbell, Philip Converse, Warren Miller and Donald Stokes, *The American Voter* (New York: Wiley, 1967), pp. 223–30; and Duncan Macrae Jr., *Parliament, Parties and Society in France, 1946–1958* (New York: St. Martin's Press, 1967), Ch. 9.
52. Parodi, op. cit., pp. 60–1.
53. See Robert Lane, *Political Life* (New York: Free Press, 1959), pp. 261–4; and Robert Putnam, 'Political Attitudes and the Local Community,' *American Political Science Review*, **60**, No. 3 (1966).
54. Pronier, op. cit., is particularly good in analyzing the entrenchment of the party at the local level. See Part I, *passim*, as well as Chs 6 and 7 of the second part.
55. *Bulletin de l'Élu Communiste*, No. 45–6 (1973), pp. 2–3.
56. *Le Monde*, *Les Élections législatives de mars, 1978* (*Supplément aux dossiers et documents du Monde*, mars 1978), p. 76.
57. See Elisabeth Dupoirier and Gérard Grunberg, 'Vote municipal et vote legisliatif,' *Revue Française de Science Politique*, **22**, No. 2, April 1972, p. 267. The findings can be compared if we consider the somewhat different sample, and recalculate their table as percentages of expressed, rather than registered, voters. Also see *Le Monde*, March 21, 1978.
58. See articles by Tarrow and Milch in Blackmer and Tarrow, op. cit., pp. 164–5 and 353.
59. Parodi, op. cit., p. 60.
60. Ibid., p. 63. The linkage between national political considerations and

local elections has been stronger on the left than on the right for some time. However, linkage has gradually become more generalized on the right as well. See *Sondages*, 1978, Nos 2 and 3, pp. 86–7.

61. *Le Figaro*, February 15, 1983.

3 Policy Differences: What Do Communist-governed Cities Do?

Introduction

The impact of partisan orientation on public policy at the local level has been the subject of an extended debate among social scientists for the past twenty years. At the core of the debate is the elementary question of whether political variables in general, and partisan differences in particular, can explain differences in policy outputs: do local governments of different partisan orientations produce distinctive policy choices and priorities?

In the American context, there is some evidence that such political variables as electoral turnout and party competition are related to levels of social welfare spending, but no distinctive policy choices have been related to partisan orientation. V.O. Key, Duane Lockhart and Ira Sharkansky have argued that turnout and competition are related to higher levels of social welfare expenditure because of competition for 'low-status' votes, while one-party domination and low turnouts reduce the political impact of those with the least measure of private power.[1] However, other studies have suggested that this relationship is spurious, that it largely disappears if we control for such socio-economic variables as wealth, urban development and industrial development.[2] Although the answer to the question about the relationship between local policy outputs and political variables remains unclear — it depends on *which* political variables are chosen, and *what* we mean by policy choices (qualitative choices, spending levels per capita or spending priorities, etc.) — it does seem clear that in the United States, *partisan orientation* does not shape policy in a distinctive way at the local level.[3]

In European cities, on the other hand, we would expect partisan factors to have a more important impact on public policy outputs. This expectation is based upon both the ideological commitments and the organizational strength of European political parties.

> While Republicans, Democrats, and nonpartisan personal followings might not be expected to sponsor or produce distinctive local policy outputs, it is logical to expect greater diversity among the cities of Western Europe . . . where local government is highly politicized and where the spectrum of ideology runs from neo-Fascism through Maoism to nihilism . . . It has recently been asserted, in fact, that European cities are, at least in this sense, more democratic than American cities because of the explicit representation in urban government of the working classes and the poor by socialist and communist parties.[4]

If ideological commitment helps to focus policy priorities, organizational strength serves to enforce national priorities at the local level. Of course, there is also a presumption that there are real policy choices to be made at the local level.

In fact, the expectation that partisan orientations would be important has been borne out, although socio-economic factors, and local and regional conditions have proven to be surprisingly strong in shaping local policy. Robert Fried, for example, found that Communist strength in Italian cities was associated with conservative policies in the North and progressive policies in the South, while Christian Democratic power produced the opposite pattern. Fried points out that it is unclear if this is related to the way that the party adapted ideology to diverse cultural environments — whether it was a deliberate party strategy — or the result of a strategic choice made years ago within each city.[5] Nevertheless, if we examine the broad range of studies, the relationship between partisan orientation and policy differences in Europe appears to be important, if complex.[6]

In the case of France, we might expect this relationship to be particularly weak, given the widespread rhetoric of *apolitisme* and the general weakness of party organization at the local level (see Chapter 1). In general, parties appear to lack both the commitment and the organizational strength to develop distinctive policy choices and priorities, perhaps with the exception of the Communists. Sidney Tarrow found that only 45 percent of his sample of French mayors were members of a political party (compared with almost 90 percent of the Italian sample).[7] Of course the Communist mayors were party members, but their organizational involvement also proved to be surprisingly low: only 45 percent scored 'high' on Tarrow's index of partisan involvement. While this was three times higher than the scores of center-right mayors, it was far lower than the 76 percent score of their Italian counterparts.[8]

> The French Communist mayors had much less experience in the party organization than their Italian comrades. More than 40 percent had never held a party office higher than that of secretary of a cell or section, and almost 30 percent reported holding no party offices at all. In their comments during the interviews, PCF mayors were vigorous in their denials that they were deeply involved in the party organization. . . . It is not that organization was *un*important to the PCF mayors, with their Leninist training and instincts . . . But the PCF mayors themselves were less integrated into the party organization than their Italian Comrades.[9]

Nevertheless, French Communist local officials have expressed a will and desire to develop a distinctive kind of local government, both in terms of policies and processes. In their public statements, as well as in interviews, they have constantly stressed the importance of local government for what it can and should do, and for its importance as a microcosm of the way that policy can and should be made by Communists. In interviews, Communist mayors responded positively to the question of whether they see their 'actions' in terms of a national Communist political strategy. They generally interpreted 'actions' in terms of policy commitments, and these commitments in terms of 'obvious' priorities that were usually summarized by the expression *politique sociale* or *gestion sociale* — two phrases that can be roughly translated as policies favorable to the masses of people, by which they generally meant young people, old people, workers and (sometimes) women: 'If you like, for us to favor young people, to favor the well-being of people, is our goal as Communists. We have no need to refer to higher [party] levels in order to arrive at these priorities.'[10]

However, in a more detailed analysis of their priorities, some mayors revealed the complexities and contradictions in these commitments. Thus, the mayor of Antony asserted that certainly the local government of Antony is committed to follow the general orientation of the national PCF by 'favoring the most disinherited.' Nevertheless, the first priority is to favor an urban renewal project that would stress balanced urban development — balanced in terms of various kinds of housing, and balanced in terms of open space and public amenities. Antony has a small working-class population, and the local government appeared determined to promote the kind of growth that would preserve the existing class composition. For the mayors of Athis-Mons, Reims and Sevran, *gestion social* was understood more in process than in policy terms: 'To respond to the needs of the population means first to know them, second to respond in the best way possible, and third to use the municipal administration to effectively meet these objectives.'[11] For these mayors, a 'democratic' process clearly distinguishes their administrations from those that came before them.

Despite similar rhetoric, it is not at all clear that in their actions Communist local governments are distinctive. The will to develop distinctive programs and services can be diluted by the complexity of local needs and the variety of local priorities. Therefore, the rhetoric must be tested against the patterns of policy outputs. One measure of policy outputs is the pattern of priorities of local budgets. Existing evidence indicates that Communist-governed municipalities have been differentiated from others by the way that they have spent their money, the way they have raised money and by the way they have chosen to finance their projects.

Spending priorities

Communist-governed cities generally spend more money per

capita than cities governed by other parties. However, the difference in spending levels is modest, according to one major study, and is not statistically significant, if we control for demographic variables.[12] However, what more clearly differentiates the budgets of Communist-governed cities from others is the way that they choose to spend their money.

For example, a large percentage of the operating budgets of Communist-governed cities has been devoted consistently to school programs and to school services for children. Local governments in France have no control over school curriculum, and teachers are paid and controlled by the Ministry of Education. Nevertheless, education in general, and primary education in particular, weighs heavily on the budget of most cities. In 1973, an average of 27 percent of the operating budgets of communes in France was devoted to various education expenses, making education the most important budget item; in the larger towns these expenses surpassed a mean of 30 percent.[13] Communes were responsible for the construction, the equipment, the furniture, the materials and the upkeep of all primary and infant schools even before 1981; in addition, communes still pay most of these same expenses for secondary schools, although the state has been slowly taking over these responsibilities since 1965. Beyond these obligations, communes can also choose to enrich and supplement the educational curriculum, particularly in such areas as music, sports and nature appreciation. They can also choose to provide such social services for school children and their families as canteens, day-care centers, gymnasiums and swimming pools.[14]

Communist municipalities have given priority to this kind of spending. Although over the years the initiatives of Communist local authorities in this area have spread to other 'modern' communes, innovation in educational programs has become an identifiable characteristic of Communist government at the local level. Korbielski's study of municipal budgets (completed in 1975, but using data from 1968) found that there was a strong positive relationship between spending priorities in this area and the left-political orientation of the local government. He found that Communist local governments spent 36 percent more than non-Communist left governments, and 49 percent more than moderate/right governments per capita for education and educational support. He also found a negative relationship for such maintenance functions as road repair, lighting, street cleaning and parking facilities. Thus, Communist local governments spent 34 percent less than non-Communist left and 36 percent less than moderate-right governments for maintenance.[15]

Another way to look at the commitments of Communist-governed municipalities is to examine the changes that these governments initiate when they gain power. The most dramatic increases in spending in those cities that elected Communist mayors in 1977 were in educational services and social action. Table 3.1 includes one provincial city (Reims), three industrial towns in the Paris suburbs (Poissy, Houilles and Villeneuve-Saint-Georges), and two dormitory suburbs of Paris (Chelles and Athis-Mons). In many ways these cities are quite different, but in each case the change in government brought about a sharp increase in social spending, education and cultural spending, or both. These increases were among the largest in the budgets prepared by the new governments, and, with a few exceptions, were not equalled by increases in any other categories.

Moreover, increases in specific programs were often far greater than the general increases. For example, spending on social services in Poissy increased by only 5.3 percent, but spending on health services went up 43 percent, and the funds budgeted for the operation of the municipal crèche almost doubled. In addition, aid to senior citizens' groups was increased tenfold, and a new service of after-school care was established. Similarly, in Chelles, where funding for sports, culture and social services increased by over 50 percent, aid to sports associations tripled, and there was a massive increase of funds to the library, municipal museum and cultural center. Funding for the administration of the crèche doubled. In Houilles, the increased spending on educational services, sports and culture can be accounted for by the creation of new services for youth, sports and culture, increased funding for the municipal music school, and the establishment of after-school child care in the infant schools and the primary schools.

The increases indicated in Table 3.1 are in the operating rather than the investment budget. They reflect either the establishment of new municipal services that could not be

Table 3.1 *Percentage increases (and decreases) in spending on schools and social services in six cities that elected Communist mayors in 1977 (percentage increase from 1976 to 1978 in expense budget).*

	Chelles	*Reims*	*Athis*	*Poissy*	*Villeneuve-St-Georges*	*Houilles*
Education	+23.4%	+17.2%	+2.0%	+31.1%	−7.9%	+24.7%
Education services	+176	+47.6	−4.5	+49.6	+17.6	
Sports, music and art	+52.6	+40.1	+9.4	+21.8	+49.9	+55
Social services (health, social aid + social services)	+55.8	+48.9	+53.6	+5.3	+25.2	−4.2
Total expense budget	+23.6	+28.5	+12.4	+40.3	+26.8	+27.6

Source: *Compte administratif de l'exercice,* 1976 and 1978 for each city.

easily eliminated, or significant new commitments to existing services that could not be easily reduced. These changes are important both because they were effected so rapidly, and because they are an indication of one way that Communists who have governed at the local level conceive of change. Despite some variation from city to city, these changes also reveal a consistency that supports Korbielski's findings.[16]

If Communist local governments have chosen to spend a large proportion of their operating budgets on the development and financing of social and educational programs, Korbielski found that they have also chosen to pay for these programs largely out of tax money collected locally. Taxes paid in these communes were higher than those paid in others. Korbielski calculated that while the operating budgets of the Communist communes were 13 percent higher than those of other communes, they collected 26 percent more taxes. While spending differences are not statistically significant, tax differences are.[17] This money was spent on financing municipal operations and services. Thus, non-Communist municipalities have tended to pay out of tax revenues for a high proportion of the operating expenses of those municipal functions that they favor, financing the expenses of other functions with higher fees for services. Communist governments, according to Korbielski, have tended to support both favored and less-favored functions with tax revenues rather than fees for services.[18]

However, an examination of the financing patterns of recently-elected Communist governments indicates that financing patterns do not change quickly or easily. In general, the method of financing key municipal functions has changed very little with the change of government, and patterns have tended to resemble those of previous budgets far more than they have resembled each other. Moreover, there has been increasing concern expressed among Communist mayors about the rapidly rising level of local taxes, and for certain (particularly new) services and facilities, they have turned to graduated fees for services, rather than increased taxes.

Poissy, for example, had provided an extensive network of social services for its school children under the government before 1977 that was, of course, maintained by the new Communist-led government. While spending in this area was increased by almost 50 percent, and much of the increase was related to spending on food for the canteen, the pattern of financing this expenditure was similar under both governments: about 30 percent of the revenue came from fees and payments from those who used the services — mostly payments to the canteen. The pattern was also maintained in Reims. Spending increased by almost 50 percent, and the financing pattern was also maintained. However, in Reims, fees and payments accounted for only 15 percent of the revenues.

Changes in financing patterns have sometimes been related to the establishment of new facilities but not always in ways anticipated. The new government in Chelles opened a new canteen for school children, and financed it largely out of the fees paid by those who used it. Similarly, Poissy built new sports facilities and a new swimming pool, and financed their use out of entrance fees. In both cases, the percentage of the budget of these services covered by tax revenues declined dramatically. Other changes in financing reveal altered priorities and preferences about which services should be subsidized from tax revenues. Chelles, for example, doubled its spending on the municipal crèche, but also doubled its revenues from fees. On the other hand, the city vastly increased spending on the municipal swimming pool, but *lowered* its income from entrance fees.

Finance patterns appear to have changed far less frequently and far less consistently than spending patterns in those municipalities that changed political direction in 1977, at least in the short run. This probably reflected the political difficulty of increasing local taxation. In general, Communist-led governments have been reluctant to impose heavy new tax burdens on an already 'overburdened population,' and therefore have sought to pay for their new programs in other ways.

While the *level* of direct taxes collected by localities is decided locally (the number of 'centimes'), the *proportion* of direct taxes paid by households, landowners and businesses was fixed by the state according to a complex formula. Under legislation passed in 1980, municipalities gained the limited right to alter the proportions of direct taxes as well as the levels, except for business taxes, which effectively remained under the control of the state. Business taxes (*la taxe professionelle*) depend upon the extent and the earnings of business and industry in a town. However, this limited flexibility has been further limited and reduced, even while the government of the left has been implementing decentralization legislation.[19]

It has been argued that since so many Communist-governed cities are heavily industrialized, the proportion of direct taxes paid by business is very high. This permits these cities to raise more tax revenue, with fewer political consequences, and with greater redistributive impact.[20] However, in analyzing figures released by the Ministry of the Interior, we found that for cities over 30,000, the mean percentage of direct taxes covered by the business tax was 53 percent, while the mean percentage of Communist-governed cities was 55 percent. In fact there was only a small variation among the groups of cities governed by different parties (52 percent for both the non–Communist left and the moderate right).[21] Variation within the Communist and non-Communist groups of cities was also roughly similar, indicating that the options with regard to taxation were also similar.

Therefore, it would be too simple to explain the higher

spending of Communist-governed municipalities in terms of their ability to raise revenues from business taxes. If the tax level is increased, the consequences are similar for households in Communist and non-Communist-governed towns. Even where the percentage of direct taxes paid by businesses is high the willingness of new Communist-led governments to increase taxes has varied considerably.

In Béziers per capita direct taxes increased almost 90 percent between 1977 and 1980. 'It is a choice . . . One does not make social [policy] without a financial counterpart, without higher taxes.'[22] Almost half of the increased tax burden was covered by the business tax. Poissy, however, where 70 percent of the direct taxes are covered by the business tax, raised its per capita tax burden only 6 percent in two years. In both cities, the annual increase of the operating budget was about the same. The problem of how to finance expanded public services was far more serious, however, for cities like Chelles or Athis-Mons that have a small industrial base, and collect only 40 percent of their direct tax revenues from businesses.

Chelles provides an interesting example of some of the restricted choices that were made to finance a 25 percent increase in two years of the operating budget. The centrist government that held power until 1977 chose a lower level of services that could be paid for mostly out of tax revenues, state subsidies and low fees for services. The new Communist-led government after 1977 chose to expand services (see above), but with higher fees to cover additional costs.

Prior to the 1977 election, Chelles provided free local bus services, paid for out of local revenues, with some subsidy derived from fines for traffic violations. The total cost to the municipality was over two million francs a year. After the elections, the new council decided to reorganize the urban transit system, and to finance the system largely out of fares collected. The 1978 budget called for a municipal expenditure of only 700,000 francs. At the same time, spending on education and social services was vastly increased over previous budgets (as noted above), both absolutely (168 percent over 1976), and relatively (7.3 percent of the operating budget as opposed to 3.5 percent in 1976), but here, too, fees would cover a far greater proportion of the expense. (See Table 3.2.) Thus the increase was financed, more or less equally, by tax revenue and fee revenue.

Table 3.2 *Percentage of direct expenses covered by means other than taxes*

	Chelles		*Reims*		*Athis*		*Poissy*	
	1976	*1978*	*1976*	*1978*	*1976*	*1978*	*1976*	*1978*
Education	12%	14%	26%	19%	32%	60%	6%	9%
Education services	15	56	18	17	64	54	72	66
Sports, music and art	39	14	7	6	10	7	6	26
Social services (health, social aid + social services)	10	16	17	13	50	30	30	34

Source: *Compte administratif de l'exercice*, 1976 and 1978 for each city.

The social impact of these measures was offset, to a certain extent, by the establishment of a sliding scale for fees and special fares on urban transit for the less privileged. However, the primary concern of the mayor and the municipal council was to hold the tax rates down in a city where most of the tax bill was paid by 'ordinary people.' Bourdu, the mayor of Chelles, carefully emphasized before the municipal council that the principal injustice was the high level of taxes paid by families in order to subsidize those who rode public transportation — '35,000 inhabitants support the transit charges without using any urban transport . . . The users will pay like everyone else; on the other hand, citizens will benefit from a decrease in taxes.'[23]

The example provided by Chelles is extraordinary in the sense that it is a Communist-governed municipality that has decided to expand fees for services in some areas, rather than maintain the 'social' payments for services followed by the centrist government that it followed. It is also a good example of how a *politique sociale* can be interpreted in different ways, particularly when it comes to financing programs in different tax structures. It appears that the pattern that Korbielski found for financing various municipal functions is not a particularly good guide for understanding the priorities of change that newly established Communist-led municipalities have set for themselves.

There is stronger evidence, however, that Communist-governed municipalities have made clearer and more consistent choices about financing their investments. Compared to other municipalities, those governed by Communists have sought to finance their investments with loans and grants, rather than self-financing. Jerome Milch found that while Montpellier (then governed by a moderate coalition) financed more than a third of its investment through savings drawn from its operating budget, Nîmes, with a Communist government, financed only about 20 percent of its investment this way, relying heavily on government loans for the rest.[24] Montpellier, by spending more of its direct revenue on investment, kept its debt low and reduced its reliance on the state. Its population paid for this in other ways, however, because this mode of financing reduced the amount of money available for operating functions, and because users of services paid more in fees. Jean Montaldo, using a 1974 survey of middle-sized cities in three provincial regions, found that relative to taxes collected, self-financing was three times higher in Montpellier than in Nîmes. In general, self-financing for non-Communist cities was about two-thirds higher than for Communist-governed cities.[25]

In the sample of cities that we used in Tables 3.1 and 3.2, we found, in four of five budgets submitted for 1978, either a continuation of a policy of outside financing for investment (in the case of Chelles), or (in the case of Reims, Poissy and Athis-Mons) a sharp drop in self-financing, relative to revenues. (See Table 3.3.) This drop is quite significant because it was effected so quickly. While Poissy and Servan generally maintained their previous levels of investment, the investment programs in the other towns were significantly increased. Therefore, Communist-governed municipalites have chosen to increase their dependence on the state by increasing their loan and grant applications in order to maintain and/or increase their investments.

Thus far we have examined some of the ways that Communist-governed municipalities can be differentiated from other local governments in policy terms. They are distinctive in their choice of services they attempt to supply; there is some evidence that they are distinctive in the ways that they pay for these services; and they are distinctive in the way

Table 3.3 *Investment choices in six Communist-governed cities (1976 and 1978)*

	Loans and grants as percentage of investment finance		*Self-finance as percentage of revenue*		*Social investment as percentage of communal investment*	
	1976	*1978*	*1976*	*1978*	*1976*	*1978*
Chelles	61%	82%	—	—	26%	63%
Reims	87	89	8%	5%	41	39
Athis	12	68	10	2	11	37
Poissy	60	89	18	7	39	65
Villeneuve-Saint-Georges	72	87	18	-3	94	55
Sevran	98	82	—	6	—	—

Source: *Compte administratif de l'exercice*, 1976 and 1978 for each city.

that they finance their investments, relying more upon the state than on their own resources. It is also easier to generalize about policy choices in Communist-governed cities than in those governed by other parties. Korbielski found that variation among Communist-governed cities with regard to budget priorities is considerably less than among other party groups. Deviation from the pattern in the Communist group tends to occur among the smaller towns, outside of the Paris region, where the mayor may be less integrated into the party structure and the interaction among Communist local officials. For cities governed by the non-Communist left and the center, those that deviate the most from the mean of their group tend to be centers of large agglomerations, where the mayor is most likely to be an important notable, not easily influenced by party considerations.[26]

If we can identify and differentiate similar policy choices in cities governed by Communist mayors, we can presume that these choices reflect local political priorities or national PCF priorities rather than central government priorities, unless these localities are sufficiently similar that our findings simply reflect central state distribution to a particular kind of locality. This, however, does not seem to be the case, as we saw in Chapter 2. Differences in policy priorities (and similarities) that mark Communist-governed cities, particularly policies that require considerable support from central authorities, are a good measure of the ability of localities to make autonomous choices, and mobilize resources from the center. The choices that they have made are most evident in their budgets in these policy areas. However, there are other choices that Communist-governed municipalities have made that are less evident in an analysis of their operating and investment budgets, choices that are more 'qualitative' than quantitative, such as in the areas of housing, urban planning and urban development, and immigrant policy.

In these areas, the policies of Communist governments have been historically different from those of other governments, although in recent years much of this distinctiveness has been obscured. What remains distinctive is the extent and the depth of their involvement in these areas rather than the social quality and distinctiveness of the policies themselves. An analysis of these policies nevertheless provides an insight into the political importance of some of the cumulative social changes in Communist-governed cities.

Housing and urban development

Communist local governments have taken a strong interest in housing policy, particularly subsidized, low-income public housing. Public housing is neither constructed nor managed directly by local authorities in France. In general, the responsibility for such housing is in the hands of an independent *Office d'habitations à loyer modéré* (OHLM), which is established at the local or departmental level, and whose members are responsible to and appointed by the prefect. Nevertheless, local officials can influence the makeup of the HLM councils, can lower the ultimate rental costs of HLM-built housing, and can sponsor additional housing by supporting construction by non-commercial groups.

Localities in general, and Communist-governed cities in particular, appear to have little difficulty influencing appointments to the administrative councils for the HLM offices;[27] HLM offices have come to reflect the broad housing policies of the localities within their jurisdictions with regard to the expansion of public housing, the rents that are charged and the selection of applicants for apartments.

Communist municipalities are reputed to have pursued policies that have favored the expansion of low-rental public housing. Indeed, through the decade of the 1960s, public housing proliferated in most of the large Communist-governed towns. Milch found that between 1959 and 1970, Nîmes built 9,500 units, twice the number of neighboring Montpellier.[28] During the same period, new, high-rise public housing was built by OHLMs throughout the 'red belt' of Paris. In one of the few attempts to analyze the distribution of public housing, and the population living in public housing, it was found that in 1975, in the working-class suburbs of Paris, almost a third of the total population lived in HLMs.[29] By comparison, in the city of Paris, only 10 percent of the population lived in public housing in 1975. Eighty-six percent of the public housing residents in the Paris region live in the suburbs.[30]

The commitment of Communist municipalities to public housing in the 1970s is also indicated by the way it was financed. The ultimate rents in subsidized public housing are a reflection of the costs of constructing the units, and there is evidence that Communist-controlled offices have attempted to finance construction in ways that will keep costs down and that will minimize direct expenses to the municipality. Thus, an annual government report stressed in 1976 that certain Communist-controlled offices have relied most heavily for financing on long-term loans from the ministry of construction and housing, and far less on self-financing and financial contributions of the municipality.[31] Milch stressed that, in contrast to Montpellier, Nîmes was willing to reduce the ultimate cost of public housing by providing the HLM office with cheap land (priced below the market value) and cheap services, such as roads, sewage and street lighting. In addition, Nîmes has had a relatively liberal policy towards underwriting housing construction by private companies. 'The primary concern of local authorities in Nîmes . . . has been the "social utility" of the proposed construction. If the project seems worthwhile, they have been willing to provide a guarantee regardless of financial considerations.'[32] This kind of policy has been followed frequently by other Communist-governed municipalities, and, as a result, they have sometimes been forced to pay lending institutions when private construction groups have defaulted.[33]

Although precise figures are difficult to obtain, administrators from the ministry of housing, Communist local officials and critics of Communist local governments all agree that during the 1960s, Communist municipalities either initiated and/or acquiesced in a vast expansion of public housing units in their towns. In fact, no one disputes that *couleur politique* is a good index for calculating the level of public housing in a commune.

The choice to build and to administer a large amount of public housing has been frequently attributed to the desire of Communist local governments to perpetuate a counter-community and to strengthen the party organization. Thus, they have been accused of giving preference for apartments to members of the PCF, and of encouraging the construction of low-income housing in order to concentrate Communist voters in specific locations. Their purpose is reputed to be both electoral and organizational:

> I invite those who still believe that a Communist municipality is well governed, and that it is committed to the satisfaction of the needs of all of its inhabitants to visit Corbeil-Essonnes, 'occupied' for 18 years by a Communist government. Its administration obeys the following principals found in all of the Communist municipalities, for they are imposed by the Central Committee of the Communist Party:
>
> 1. Construction *en masse* of HLMs, whatever the local needs, to the exclusion of all other types of housing.
> 2. Priority for apartments for those who hold party cards. That permits the increase of Communist Party electors, often by making them come from other localities, while discouraging others.[34]

Formally, there are objective criteria for admission into public housing units — the order of candidates on a list, and the number of years that a candidate has resided within a commune, as well as whether the applicant is currently living in habitable housing. Within these criteria, those governmental units (and private institutions) that participate in the construction of HLMs may choose among the applicants. In practice, however, the rules are often bent and informally other criteria are frequently applied.

Interviews with local officials confirm that Communist militants have been encouraged to live in *cités HLM*, and that the party has concentrated much of its recruitment in these projects (local officials frequently acknowledge that they were recruited into the party *after* they moved to HLM projects). However, until recently, cities governed by the left in general, and by the Communists in particular, have been constrained (more by their own ideological commitments than by any master-plan to increase their electoral support) to bear the brunt of the demographic changes in the urban areas of the country. As the inner cities have become increasingly gentrified, more and more immigrant workers, unskilled workers, retired people, and young people with large families have been pushed into the inner suburbs, particularly into those suburban towns that have been willing to accept low-income housing — towns governed by the left.[35]

Thus, while political criteria for selection for public housing have not been absent, a more important result of both the decision to build public housing, and the selection process of the HLM boards, has been a rapid influx into Communist-governed municipalities of the most disfavored workers and their families, many of whom are immigrants (who do not have the right to vote). Although through the 1970s Communist-governed municipalities could be distinguished by their encouragement of public housing, they could also be distinguished by their disproportionately high levels of immigrant workers and their families.

From the perspective of the locality, the decision to expand public housing during the 1960s appeared to be more a somewhat panicked response to pressing needs than a calculated electoral or organizational plan. The experience of Vitry with low-income housing is instructive. This classic bastion, whose mayor until 1978 was Marcel Rosette, PCF spokesman for local government problems, has been governed by Communists since 1925. A private municipal report, circulated among local government officials in 1973, notes that the municipal council '. . . decided to support the construction of an important number of low-income housing units (in 1954) in order to respond to the needs created by the demographic growth of the city.'[36] After nine years of protracted negotiations for financing with various organisms of the state, construction was finally begun in 1963. The report insists that the key issue was the percentage of low-income housing relative to the total number of units. It goes on to indicate some of the painful choices that were made:

> This plan, which integrates a large proportion of low-income housing, necessitated the maximum utilization of land, in order to reduce the charges per apartment. For at that time, land speculation caused prices to rise. That led to denser construction ... This was the unfavorable aspect of the compromise, an aspect that we question most strongly today, but that was necessary at the time, if we wanted to construct social housing in spite of the financial disengagement of the state.[37]

The report goes on to argue that the compromise made in 1963 is directly responsible for widespread discontent and unhappiness among those residents of the housing already constructed, and calls for a halt in new construction (of private units), an expansion of services, and an increase in the use of land for parks, parking and community activities.

The shift in priorities by Vitry in 1973 is reflected in the choices made by those cities with new Communist mayors in 1977. In general, they appear to be far more committed to balanced urban development than either their non-Communist predecessors, or than their party colleagues had been in the past. Vitry is constantly presented as an example of urban failure by many of these new mayors, although they also recognize that the demographic pressures of the 1980s are quite different from those of the 1960s. Even now, however, the mayor of Chelles mused that, while it would not be desirable to build more low-income housing in Chelles, five or six hundred units would have to be constructed during the next five years to cover a thousand requests. Nevertheless, in Chelles, as in other towns, it is now evident that more complex choices are now being made. These choices can be seen more clearly if housing is considered in the context of urban planning and urban development. In this context, we can assess both the changes in policies among the Communist local authorities, and the differences between the choices made by Communist and non-Communist governments, since urban planning priorities were a major issue in a number of cities where Communist-led lists were successful in 1977.

In the nine Communist-governed municipalities where I interviewed intensively a year after the new governments came to power, housing and urban planning had been a major issue in the election campaigns of four, and an important issue in three others. The general concern was with urban sprawl, and poorly planned, 'inhuman' housing. Clearly, the expansion of housing was important in all of these cases, and the former governments were sharply criticized for planning housing in such a way that access for low-income renters would be difficult. However, there were other considerations that were at least as important.

In two cities (Athis-Mons and Antony) in the Paris region, plans had already been approved for the destruction or major renovation of an older center-city area. Prior to the election of 1977 in Athis-Mons, Communist and Socialist militants had blocked the bulldozers that were about to begin renovation. The very first day that the new municipal council met, on March 25, 1977, it suspended application of the construction plans in the development zone. Within a year, the city government was able to renegotiate the plans. In Antony, the development plan of the previous government had been far more broadly conceived, and was integrated into the general zoning plan (the POS) that had already been approved by the prefect. During their first year in office, the new local government undertook a major revision of the POS, while continuing negotiations with the field services of the ministry of equipment for permission to implement the changes. As in Athis-Mons, expansion of low-income housing (and the facilities to serve that housing) were important considerations, but the major revisions concerned the preservation of the older center-city area.

In Sevran, also in the Paris region, massive reconstruction of the city-center was already in progress, and bitterly opposed by the incoming Communist–Socialist coalition. Here, the new government pledged to modify what it could to save what was left of the core of the center-city, and to preserve and improve the older one- and two-family homes. Their plans did not call for any expansion of low-income housing. During the first year in office, the modification of the urban plan was still under consideration. The major concern was the size of the buildings being constructed, as well as the lack of provision for green space and communal institutions in the existing plan. These were also the principal concerns that motivated changes in zoning and construction plans in two other cities in the Paris region — Houilles and Villeneuve-Saint-Georges. In Houilles, the municipal government was most concerned with the ratio of proposed low-income housing to green space, and the mayor of Villeneuve insisted that the new municipal government had altered the zoning plan to prevent the development of 'another Vitry.' Local officials in Antony and Sevran also used Vitry as a negative example.

Communist government and the politics of race

This emphasis upon balanced urban development should also be seen in terms of the changing social structure of Communist-governed municipalities (see Chapter 2). The mixed profile is accentuated by the fact that many of the diminished number of working-class residents of these cities are working-class immigrants, who are not fully accepted, and who do not vote. In 1975, 55 percent of the Communist-governed cities had immigrant populations greater than 10 percent, compared with 24 percent of the towns with Socialist mayors and 24 percent of those with centrist mayors. The mean percentage of immigrants in Communist-governed cities was over 11 percent, compared with 7 percent for the others. There is evidence, moreover, that the immigrant population is increasing in Communist-governed towns.[38] (See Table 3.4.) In effect, this has meant that a large percentage of the working-class population in these towns is an immigrant proletariat, and as this population has increased, policies most favorable to the working-class population have tended to diminish in importance, particularly housing policies. Thus, the emphasis upon balanced urban development, which has meant fewer units of public, subsidized housing, has corresponded with doubling of the immigrant population in public housing in the Paris region.[39]

Table 3.4 *The number of cities governed by different political parties by concentration of immigrant population*

% Immigrant population (1975)	*Party of mayor (1982)*					
	Communist		*Socialist Non-communist left*		*Center-right*	
	–	%	–	%	–	%
-10%	33	45	62	77	49	79
10.1–20%	35	47	18	22	13	21
20.1%+	6	8	1	1	0	0
Total	74	100	81	100	62	100
Mean immigrant population for each group (%)	11.5		7.0		7.1	

Source: The percentage of immigrants is derived from 1975 census figures. The political breakdown is as of 1982.

The changing approach to housing policy is demonstrated most dramatically in the case of Venissieux, the working-class suburb of Lyon, governed by Communist mayors since 1936. In 1965, the city government cooperated in planning the largest public housing complex in the country. After the first year of construction, the city boasted that it had assured both low cost housing for workers, as well as sufficient social and cultural facilities, and, after the first buildings were occupied, the municipal government reminded voters that:

> To construct social housing is a political choice. Venissieux has preferred to see constructed housing for the least favored social categories, has shared in the expenses of construction of a large number of [these apartments], and in the same way, has assumed responsibility for the expenses that this leads to [facilities of every kind, welfare aid, school buildings, etc.][40]

By 1975, half the population of Venissieux lived in the new complex — Les Minguettes. However, the demand for public housing among French workers began declining during the 1970s, while the demand was growing among immigrant worker families, particularly those from North Africa. Thus, by 1977, two-thirds of those who lived in Les Minguettes were immigrants, two-thirds of whom were from Third World countries.[41] Although half the population of Venissieux was considered working class by the census, only 30 percent (perhaps less) were native working class. As the number of foreign residents increased, the municipal authorities began to pressure the various housing authorities that controlled Les Minguettes to refuse apartments to immigrants (as well as Third World French citizens), even if this meant that apartments would remain empty. Thus, by 1982, 25 percent of the apartments were empty, not because of the flight of French families and not because there was no demand from workers, but because after 1977, 'under pressure from the city, a consensus was established to refuse [apartments to] new immigrant households . . . The refusal of apartments not only to foreign households, but also to migrants of French nationality, closed even more any possibility of maneuver.'[42] In 1982, the housing authorities, with the full agreement of the municipal government, decided to demolish at least one of the apartment towers of Les Minguettes.[43]

Therefore, although some Communist-governed municipalities have responded to demographic changes in their constituencies by accentuating the priority of balanced urban development, others, such as Venissieux, have moved towards balance in housing by excluding foreign workers and their families from the 'least favored social categories.' Still others have moved in a more direct way towards excluding and restricting immigrants from the special services normally available to workers in a Communist-governed city.

In 1978, Ivry, the Communist-governed suburb of Paris, abandoned the traditional distribution of used clothing to deprived families when it was discovered that 80 percent of those receiving clothing were the children of immigrants.[44] In January 1981, the same city announced that a quota of 15 percent would be applied to children of immigrant families for the city's summer camps, normally open to all children living in the city. Immigrant children are 28 percent of the population under the age of sixteen, and a much higher percentage of the children from the poorest families. The municipal authorities argued that in some summer camps, immigrant children comprised half the children in camp, and that the purpose of the quota was 'to limit and push back the weight of immigration.'[45]

In the Paris region, perhaps as a result of a more general Communist campaign against immigrants in 1980–1, several letters were sent by Communist local authorities rejecting the applications of immigrants from French overseas territories (who are, of course, French citizens) specifically on racial grounds. One letter from the housing office of Saint-Denis noted that there was a quota:

> the administrative council has decided to house only native families ... [because of] the saturation in our district of applications by foreign families and families from the overseas departments and territories.[46]

A second, from Nanterre, argued on other grounds:

> We are constrained to limit the housing of persons originating in the overseas territories. In effect, their presence in our buildings provokes numerous problems at different levels ... their way of living — frequent and late gatherings, loud shouting and loud music.[47]

In effect, over a long period of time, Communist local authorities while welcoming immigrant workers into their communities as 'victims of social discrimination' in the late 1960s, gradually began to see them as a burden imposed by the state.[48] As early as 1969, the Communist mayors of the Paris region protested against the inequitable distribution of immigrant workers and their families.[49] By the late 1970s, the formal protests had deteriorated into crude actions directed against both immigrants and French workers from overseas territories in particular cities, and during the presidential campaign of 1981 these actions emerged as a coordinated campaign led by the national leaders of the Communist Party.[50]

Thus, it appears that if Communist-governed municipalities can be distinguished from those governed by other parties by their commitment to public housing and social services, they can also be distinguished by their discriminatory policies towards immigrant workers and their families who were attracted by these policies. However, this conclusion is not so clear. City governments of all political persuasions have reacted strongly against concentrations of immigrant families within their borders, in much the same way as those governed by Communists. What has distinguished Communist municipalities has been the coordination of many of their actions in recent years.

The demolition of housing in Communist-governed Venissieux to disperse concentrations of immigrants has been under way in neighboring (Socialist) Villeurbanne since 1977, under a plan first developed by the former (centrist) municipal government. Moreover, the attempt to restrict the number of immigrants in public housing through quotas has become accepted throughout the Lyon region. Indeed, under pressure from local authorities, the prefect of the department issued a circular recommending that new immigrants be prevented from moving into any neighborhood where 45 percent or more of the children in the local elementary school are immigrants.[51] Throughout the country, local authorities, regardless of political party, have refused to admit immigrants into public housing, and, above all, have systematically refused the construction of dormitories for single workers.[52]

When the Communist mayor of Vitry led a group of municipal councilors together with a group of 'irate' citizens in a march against a newly-installed immigrant workers' dormitory during the 1981 presidential campaign, the actions were widely, but not universally condemned. The Socialist group in Vitry supported what had been done, as did other local officials from towns with high concentrations of immigrants.[53] Moreover, almost every side of the 'debate' accepted the definition of the issue — if not the solution — of the Communists, that immigrant concentration posed problems of racial/ethnic conflict.[54]

Also, it is important to understand that the policies of Communist-governed municipalities have been variable and inconsistent. At the same time that local governments were engaged in the actions and policies that we described above, they were also providing aid and advice to immigrants in their struggles against expulsions from public housing and dormitories as well as legal help against the state that enabled many immigrants to remain in France.[55]

What most distinguishes Communist municipalities from those governed by other parties is their involvement with the issue of immigrants, rather than the policies that they have pursued, and by and large, their policies in this area have reflected the ambiguities of this more intense involvement. Policy in this area also reflects the way that the issue has developed. While the explosive actions during the presidential campaign showed that the local issues were dictated from the center of the Communist Party, the evidence presented above indicates that in at least some Communist-governed municipalities these issues have been building for some time.

Conclusion

In this chapter we have analyzed some of the differences between policy choices made by Communist-governed municipalities and those governed by mayors of other parties. We have also looked at choices and priorities that have changed over time, as well as some of the different approaches that have developed among Communist-governed cities.

In their broadest outlines, we have found that policies in these cities are characterized by similarities in the kinds of priorities that those who govern them have established, priorities that can be differentiated from those in cities governed by other parties. Thus, there is substance to the claims by Communists that their policy choices are different. However, we have also found that within these broad outlines there are some important differences and changes over time, differences that qualify the monolithic image portrayed in the writing of the detractors of Communist local government.

We have also found that the kinds of policy choices that Communist local authorities have made almost invariably increase their dependency upon the central state and the cooperation of the central administration, which, during the period of this study, was under the control of their political opponents. Thus, while they have frequently complained about the long arm and the heavy weight of the state during the Fifth Republic, Communist local authorities more than others have made choices that have deeply involved them with central decision-makers. Different policy choices therefore indicate some differences in center–periphery relations that are characteristic of Communist-governed cities. School services, many social services, public housing and choices for urban development have not been imposed by central authorities on larger communes, but they have been initiated by localities, and then weighed against national priorities and criteria for funding.

Therefore, the range of new programs, changes in old programs as well as new investments that have been initiated by Communist-governed municipalities are an indication of one dimension of local power — the relative autonomy of local decision-making. The extent to which these initiatives have been successful is a fair indication of a second dimension of local power — influence over central decision-making. The ability of Communist-governed municipalities to extract benefits from central authorities and the structures and processes through which they have developed autonomous choices are analyzed in the next chapter.

Notes

1. See V.O. Key, *Southern Politics* (New York: Knopf–Vintage, 1949), pp. 298–310; Duane Lockhart, *New England State Politics* (Princeton: Princeton University Press, 1959), pp. 320–40; Ira Sharkansky and Richard Hofferbert, 'Dimensions of State Politics, Economics and Public Policy,' *American Political Science Review*, **53**, No. 3, September 1969, p. 868; Edmond Fowler, 'Reformism and Public Policies in American Cities,' *American Political Science Review*, **61**, No. 3, September 1967.
2. Richard Dawson and James Robinson, 'Inter-party Competition, Economic Variables and Welfare Policies in American States,' *Journal of Politics*, **25**, No. 2, May 1963, p. 265; and Thomas Dye, *Politics, Economics and the Public: Policy Outcomes in the American States* (Chicago: Rand McNally, 1966).
3. Ibid. This argument is summarized by Robert Fried, *Comparative Urban Performance*, Working Paper No. 1, European Urban Research, UCLA, 1975.
4. Robert Fried, 'Party and Policy in West German Cities,' *American Political Science Review*, **70**, No. 1, March 1976, p. 12. Many of the comparative findings are summarized in Michael Aiken and Roger Depre, 'Politics and Policy in Belgian Cities,' Western Societies' Program, Occasional Paper No. 9, Center for International Studies, Cornell University, April 1978.
5. Robert Fried, 'Communism, Urban Budgets, and the Two Italies: A Case Study in Comparative Urban Government,' *Journal of Politics*, November 1971, pp. 1,049–51.

6. Aiken and Depre, op. cit., pp. 5 and 6.
7. Sidney Tarrow, *Between Center and Periphery* (New Haven: Yale University Press, 1977), p. 127.
8. Sidney Tarrow, 'Party Activists in Public Office: Comparisons at the Local Level in Italy and France,' in Donald Blackmer and Sidney Tarrow, eds, *Communism in Italy and France* (Princeton: Princeton University Press, 1975), p. 147.
9. Ibid.
10. May or of Villeneuve-Saint-Georges, May 1978.
11. Mayor of Reims, May 8, 1978.
12. José Korbielski, 'Tendence politique des municipalités et comportements financiers locaux' (paper presented at the conference on Politics, Policy and the Quality of Urban Life, Ballagio, Italy, June 1975), p. 6.
13. *Le Monde de l'Éducation*, March 1977, p. 7. In 1973, communes spent 22 percent of the budget of the ministry of education.
14. Ibid., pp. 7–14.
15. Korbielski, 'Tendence . . . ,' p. 9. Also, see José Korbielski, 'L'Influence de la structure des communes urbaines sur leurs dépenses de fonctionnement' (doctoral dissertation, Université de Rennes, 1975), pp. 310–12.
16. These findings have also been supported by other investigations. See the series of articles on *union-de-gauche* municipalities in *Le Monde*, April 8–12, 1980, especially the article on Béziers on April 12.
17. Korbielski, 'Tendence . . . ,' p. 22.
18. Ibid., p. 24.
19. See Raymond Pronier, *Les Municipalités communistes* (Paris: Balland, 1983), pp. 233–4. For a review of changes in municipal financing, see Commission du Bilan, *La France en mai, 1981*, Vol. 5, *L'État et les citoyens* (Paris: La Documentation Française, 1981), pp. 296–7.
20. Jean Montaldo, *Les Finances du PCF* (Paris: Albin Michel, 1977), pp. 14–18.
21. See *Évolution de la fiscalité directe locale, 1976* (Paris: Ministère de l'Intérieur, direction générale des collectivités locales, 1977).
22. The mayor of Béziers, cited in *Le Monde*, April 12, 1980.
23. Minutes of the Municipal Council, session of March 29, 1978, pp. 4–5.
24. Jerome Milch, 'Influence as Power: French Local Government Reconsidered,' *British Journal of Political Science*, 4 (1974), pp. 143–5.
25. Jean Montaldo, *La France communiste* (Paris: Albin Michel, 1978), pp. 140–1.
26. Korbielski, 'L'Influence . . .,' pp. 310–12.
27. Montaldo, op. cit., pp. 165–75, and Milch, op. cit., pp. 148–52.
28. Ibid., p. 149.
29. Michel Pinçon, *Les Immigrés et les HLM* (Paris: Centre de Sociologie Urbaine, 1981), p. 119.
30. Ibid., p. 118.
31. Cour de Comptes, *Rapport au Président de la République, 1976*, cited by Montaldo, op. cit., p. 174. The report did not allude specifically to Communist-run offices. However, all of the offices it mentioned were in fact Communist run.

32. Milch, op. cit., p. 150.
33. Montaldo, op. cit., pp. 174–5, citing the 1976 report of the Cour de Comptes; however, this has not been a problem only for Communist-governed cities. See Cour de Comptes, *Rapport . . ., 1978*, pp. 56–9.
34. Serge Dassault, candidate for the 'majority' list in the 1977 municipal elections in Corbeil-Essonnes, quoted in *Le Figaro*, March 16, 1977. Dassault's list lost.
35. Manuel Castells, 'Planification urbaine et mouvements sociaux: Le cas de renovation urbaine à Paris,' in Colloques nationaux de CNRS, *L'Analyse Interdisciplinaire de la Croissance Urbaine* (Paris: CNRS, 1972).
36. This internal report (1974), entitled *Le Grand Ensemble*, attempts to explain the origins of the urban renewal project, and the compromise with the ministry of equipment in 1963. Tall apartment towers were constructed to reduce the charges per apartment, but the social consequences were 'disastrous.' See p. 1.
37. Ibid., p. 3.
38. See Martin A. Schain, 'Immigrants and Politics in France,' in John Ambler, ed, *France Under Socialist Leadership* (Philadelphia: Institute for the Study of Human Issues, 1984).
39. Véronique de Rudder, 'La Crise de l'habitat social ou naissance des ghettos?' presented at the conference, Le logement des immigrés en France, Lille, May 13–14, 1982, p. 4, and Pinçon, op. cit., p. 61.
40. See *Venissieux, Bulletin Municipal*, November 1966, pp. 26–7 and February 1971, p. 20.
41. For the documentation of shifting housing demands, see Pinçon, op. cit., p. 59 and *Données Sociales*, Édition 1981 (Paris: ISEE, 1982), p. 68. For a detailed analysis of the problems in Les Minguettes, see *Les Minguettes, rapport presenté à la Commission pour le Dévéloppement Social des Quartiers* (Lyon: Courly-Ville de Venissieux, 1982), pp. 44, *passim*.
42. *Les Minguettes*, p. 44.
43. See Schain, 'Immigrants and Politics in France.'
44. Jean-Pierre Dumont, 'Le Racisme du Voisin,' *Le Monde*, February 14, 1981.
45. Véronique de Rudder, 'Sous les quotas, les hommes,' *Differences*, April 1981.
46. Letter from the OHLM of Saint-Denis, November 28, 1980.
47. Letter from the OHLM of Nanterre, September 20, 1980.
48. De Rudder, 'La Crise de l'habitat . . .,' p. 3.
49. See André Viergret, *Français et immigrés: le combat du PCF* (Paris: Éditions Sociales, 1975).
50. See Schain, 'Immigrants and Politics in France.'
51. Ibid.
52. Dumont, op. cit.
53. *Le Monde*, December 30, 1980.
54. Catherine Wihtol de Wenden-Didier, 'Les Immigrés et le discours politique municipal,' Colloque GRECO, Marseilles, February 18–20, 1981.
55. See Pronier, op. cit., pp. 274, 366–7, 374–7, 393–7.

4 Explaining Policy Differences: Access, Influence and Ideology

Introduction

Insofar as the policy patterns analyzed in the last chapter are different from patterns in other municipalities, how can these differences be explained? In a formally decentralized system, autonomous local initiative might be presumed, and if we were dealing with municipalities governed by parties that were part of the national majority (until 1981) dependence on access to and influence with central decision-making authorities would not be surprising. However, in centralized France, generally dominated by the center–right, the kinds of policy-initiatives made by Communist-governed municipalities, and their ability to develop these initiatives into policies raise many interesting questions.

The most obvious concern the political nature of center–periphery relations, and the ways that Communist local authorities have developed to negotiate their requests and demands in a hostile political environment. Our analysis indicated that relations between center and periphery are politicized but that the bureaucratic values that have dominated and defined these relations have in many ways given an advantage, rather than a disadvantage, to Communist local governments. Moreover, their ability to negotiate this difficult relationship is related to the kinds of requests and demands that they have made.

The patterns analyzed in the last chapter also raise questions about why and how have Communist-governed municipalities developed different kinds of policy initiatives. The most simple (and most obvious) answer would be that policies are related to party, and that these policies represent the clearest manifestation of the impact of Communist government in France. However, the source of these policy choices — while they certainly involve party — are more complex. In this chapter, we will argue that choices are related to the way that the Communists at the local level justify and legitimize their presence.

We will argue that the pattern of center–periphery relations for Communist-governed cities is somewhat different from that of other cities. Many studies have concluded that local power, while considerable in relations with the center, has been used most frequently to resist change rather than innovate.[1] Others have linked the ability to innovate to an 'extensive' *réseau relational*.[2] In the case of Communist-governed towns, the *réseau relational* is politically limited, but effective nevertheless, in securing innovative policy objectives. While there is some evidence that their contacts are better than we might expect in a hostile political environment, however, they are not better than those of cities governed by other parties, and the network of administrative contacts cannot account for their ability to develop local policy. What has most characterized and differentiated Communist-governed cities has been the way that ideology, party relations and local structure and processes have stimulated and reinforced the will for policy development. It is the will to act at the local level that has both generated policy initiatives and enhanced the ability of these localities to gain benefits from the central state.

Local–Center relations

Communist municipal authorities have generally based their electoral appeal on an inherent contradiction. On the one hand, they argued (at least until 1981) that the state is highly discriminatory and politically prejudiced in the way that it deals with them. On the other hand, they told voters that they were far more innovative and more effective in meeting the needs of their communities, as well as in extracting the necessary financing from the state. Thus the theme of the handbook issued by the municipal committee of the party central committee in 1977 is both the discriminatory weight of the state on Communist-governed cities, and the vast range of projects and programs that these municipalities offer in contrast to others.[3] Although in interviews and in public statements Communist mayors constantly reflect on the limited capacities of local governments in France, they also claim to have found a formula for greater success in gaining disproportionate aid from the discriminatory state.

> Contrary to a legend which says that when you are in opposition, you obtain less from the state, exactly the opposite actually happens. [Communist] municipalities in general obtain a maximum of subventions, a maximum of aid from all of the services, from all of the other collectivities, primarily the state . . .[4]

This statement by a Communist mayor, repeated in various ways by many other Communist mayors, appears to be somewhat exaggerated, but can be partially confirmed by empirical research. In general, there is little evidence that Communist-governed cities receive *less* in state aid than those cities governed by other parties, although this does not mean that the access of Communist local officials is as good as that of other mayors.

Access and good relations with the administration have been related to the ability of mayors to develop innovative programs and their success in gaining aid from the state. An extended *réseau relational* with the administration appears to be a prerequisite for an active and creative urban government in France. 'For every commune, whatever the party of the mayor, a network of relations is indispensible for communal equipment . . . The mayor who accomplishes the most has a network of extended relations . . .'[5] Sidney Tarrow found that more than two-thirds of those mayors claiming to have achieved important capital and/or social projects also claimed to have had a network of administrative contacts. Clearly, there is a relationship between dependence on the state for financing certain kinds of projects (particularly capital improvements) and the level of administrative contacts of mayors claiming these projects as their most important. In fact these are the very projects that Communist mayors most often claim in interviews as their most important objectives and achievements.

Mayors of the left in general, and Communist mayors in particular, appear to have a reasonably good network of contacts with the administration. However, the effectiveness of this network is usually measured by the accomplishments of the municipality it is supposed to explain.[6] When examined directly, the relationship between Communist mayors and administrative authorities is more complicated. Tarrow found that only 40 percent of the Communist mayors in his sample claimed to have medium or extensive contacts with the administration, compared with 70 percent of the whole sample.[7]

Table 4.1 *Level of administrative contacts claimed by French mayors claiming to have achieved important projects*

Most important projects	*Level of administrative contacts (%)*				
	High	*Medium*	*Low*	*Total*	*Number*
Capital building	37.5	45.8	16.7	100	24
Social services, housing	36.8	42.1	21.1	100	19
Planning and zoning	33.8	31.3	35.0	100	16

Source: Recalculated from Sidney Tarrow, *Between Center and Periphery* (New Haven: Yale University Press, 1977), p. 161.

Communist mayors interviewed for this study in 1978 and 1980 stressed the quality, rather than the extent, of administrative contacts. They frequently complained that they lacked the advantages of informal relations with government officials and administrative personnel. Relations with the prefect and subprefect, while sometimes tense, were usually cordial, but almost never easy and informal. 'The prefect must always appear non-partisan,' stressed the (then new) Communist mayor of Houilles (an industrial suburb of Paris), 'but municipal governments of the [then] majority have an old-boy system unavailable to us.' The Communist mayor of Sevran confirmed that he experienced no overt prejudice, but argued that there was a tendency of the administration to favor and to encourage the projects of the local governments of the center-right, while the mayor of Villeneuve-Saint-Georges was quick to cite numerous personal slights and acts that he perceived as discriminatory behavior.

On the other hand, Communist mayors did not generally argue that the administration discriminated against their policy proposals and against their requests for aid. Those mayors that have benefited from *cumul des mandats*, particularly those who have been deputies or senators with experience in Paris (such as the mayors of Antony, Poissy, Chelles and Reims), claimed to have made useful contacts with the administration. While they reported instances of political discrimination, they did not generalize upon them, and argued instead that the acceptance of their proposals was generally related to the quality of the dossiers that they submitted, as well as to the priorities of the government and/or the ministry involved.

Some mayors differentiated between state aid for investment and subsidies for public works. The mayor of Reims stressed that while political considerations may determine industrial investments, they do not determine the outcomes of investment requests for public projects.

> If a project conforms to existing legislation, if it meets needs, if the financial plan holds up, there is no reason to turn it down . . . Political decisions are those concerning industrial investment, not those concerning public-works projects. Tell me, are the cities of the right better equipped than those of the left in France? No — not at all!

Providing that the proposals for aid are 'solid, well prepared, straight and clear,' he claimed, there is no systematic discrimination against Reims because its mayor is a Communist.

It is clear from our interview with directors of ministerial field services and with subprefects that while (from the administrative point of view) relations with Communist mayors were 'correct,' they were also 'highly political,' and one technical advisor to the subprefect of corbeil-Esonnes noted (without being specific) that technical reasons were sometimes given to cover essentially political decisions on urban projects. However, much of the prejudice against Communist mayors appeared to be expressed in lack of access for individual favors and personal requests.

A former chief advisor to the prefect of the Essonne department confided with some exasperation that in many ways his dealings with Communist-governed municipalities were easier than with those governed by the center–right. The former presented formal requests for subventions and loans for specific projects, but the latter inundated his office with special requests for individual favors, letters and appointments.

These observations are confirmed by Ezra Suleiman, who emphasizes the use that the majority party made of the bureaucracy during the Gaullist and Giscard periods to strengthen their local bases.

> The Gaullists have used the administration in a highly partisan way, to attend to their local constituencies as well as to perform a number of political favors designed to engender electoral support for the Gaullists. Because of their persistent efforts to gain a hold on local politics approaching their hold on national affairs, the Gaullist ministers have tended to operate on the premise that their own *départements* were always to be treated as first among equals. Consequently, many Directors observed that they were at times bombarded with notes from the minister and his cabinet to see to affairs that pertained to the minister's *département*.[8]

On the other hand, Suleiman points out an aspect of administrative values that can help us to understand the kind of political access that Communist mayors have been able to secure with the central administration. One of the more enduring myths in French political life, frequently referred to by the administrative directors interviewed by Suleiman, is that the mayoral function is administrative rather than political. Therefore administrators are willing to receive and work with mayors of the opposition in ways that they are not willing to work with deputies or 'politicians.' From the perspective of the directors, contact with deputies of the opposition, especially Communists, is legitimated by their role of mayor. Thus, contrary to the usual assumptions, it is the mayoral, rather than the 'political' role that facilitates access for the *deputé-maire* of the opposition (before 1981). 'The only deputies of the PCF who had contact with the central administration were those who were also mayors, and the same was true, though to a lesser extent, of Socialist deputies.'[9]

Under specific circumstances, Suleiman points out, Communist mayors can penetrate and achieve good working relations with the central administration. When they are dealing with 'technical' matters that pertain to the commune when they have the support of *M. le Prefet*, and when they are dealing with ministries that have regional field services, mayors can develop permanent relations with civil servants representing the central administration in his department or commune. The prefect plays a central role in neutralizing the party label of the mayor, 'and may thus be able to have his own point of view championed by the mayor.'[10]

The ability of Communist mayors to penetrate the administration is probably maximized, according to Suleiman, when the local base of a minister is in the same department as the Communist-governed town. In this case, there are generally one or two officials in the minister's cabinet who are responsible for local relations, and 'will be as receptive to deputy-mayors, and even simple mayors, of the opposition as they would be to deputies or local officials of the majority.' What emerges is a tacit alliance between the minister and all of the local officials of 'his' department. Party interests remain important, but Suleiman's interviews with cabinet officials charged with local relations (generally the *chef de cabinet*) indicate that ministers have considered nurturing of personal department fiefs to be of overriding importance.

In general, however, from the point of view of central administrators, the access of Communist mayors is more limited and more conditional. It is more effective when mayors are seen most clearly in their administrative rather than their political role; when they are proposing and bargaining for programs, services and projects, not as Communists but as mayors. Therefore the shared values of the civil service correspond to the core objectives of Communist local governments and form the basis for limited working relations.

Communist mayors have also played a more active role in increasing their effectiveness in bargaining with administrative authorities. Montaldo, in his biased but interesting study of

Communist power, contends that Communist mayors have been quite effective in manipulating the administration by exploiting the same interdependence between administration and local elected officials exploited by other mayors, but perhaps with more determination and for different policy objectives.

> As for non-political administrators, the PC uses its power to influence them: it shimmers before them career advantages ('certain administrators see in us the means to release their talents'); it impresses them with its incessant applications. The activism of the PC can be explained by its will to convince those who are hesitant and those who are *attentistes*, if not by the cogency of its ideas then at least by its force.[11]

Montaldo cites the example of Arles, where the Communist local government subcontracted a great deal of its construction work to a company associated with the *Caisse des dépôts et consignations*, the principal source of loans for local governments, which in turn approved a large loan for the city.[12] In this way, Montaldo argues, the city was able to play one part of the administration against the other. Of course, this process can also be seen as active collaboration with administrative agencies for policy goals. The outcomes are not always as satisfactory for the municipality as they were in the case of Arles.

The internal report produced for the mayor of Vitry in 1973 indicates some of the complexity in this kind of bargaining. Vitry attempted to negotiate a trade-off in the early 1960s on urban renewal that was similar to that reached by Arles ten years later. In the case of Vitry the city was not able to reach an agreement with the company. Negotiations broke down (according to the report) over the small number of low-income units proposed by the general contractor, but a compromise agreement was worked out with the ministry of equipment a year later.[13] Vitry got the housing it wanted, but sacrificed what it regarded as a more desirable urban plan.

Thus, both Communist mayors and administrative officials describe local government-administrative contacts as important, limited and conditional. They are clearly better for urban development, the financing of public-works projects and the development of new services than for aid for individual requests and the promotion of industrial investment. An extended *réseau relational* may be necessary for an active and creative urban government in France, but this network seems to be more limited and more conditional for Communist local officials than for others.

Nevertheless, Communist-governed cities have probably succeeded in getting as much (or as little) in state loans per capita as other cities. During the pre-1981 period, according to Sidney Tarrow, state aid was related most closely to the rate of increase of non-agricultural employment and the rate of population increase. These relationships remained strong even when Tarrow controlled for the voting tendency of the town.[14] The success of the Communist-governed cities is perhaps more significant than for the others, both because fewer Communist mayors claimed to have extended contacts with the administration in Tarrow's sample and because of their special political burden. How then do Communist municipalities do as well as they do with their more limited access? 'How [do] they do as well as they do in capturing state resources — given the political positions of their mayors, their relative poverty in taxable resources, and the ability of the government to use the state for political purposes?'[15]

The answer to these questions can be found by shifting the analytical focus from access and *réseaux relationaux* to the content and quality of relations between Communist municipal authorities and the central state. Their relations with the state are different in a number of ways from those of other cities. Relations are based less upon the personal network of contacts of the mayor and more upon the skill of the local government in bureaucratic bargaining and maneuver. What also differentiates these cities from those analyzed in much of the literature on local government is not so much their pattern of access and their relations with the center, but the way they develop the objectives that they seek. Because of the kinds of policy priorities they have established, they are probably more dependent upon the state than other municipalities for the success of the projects and programs that they propose. On the other hand, their policy commitments do not emerge from interaction with the state administration, but are generated through a political process that is not dominated by state priorities and in which their dependency on state services is minimized.

The justification of policy at the local level

The most basic element that has differentiated Communist-governed cities from most others has been the way that they have justified holding power. On one hand, holding political power at the local level has never been an end itself, and has always been linked to national political aspirations and objectives. On the other hand, Communist local governments have always attempted to present political programs through which they could be clearly differentiated from other local governments. An examination of the way that Communist party and local officials have presented their missions, therefore, reveals their short-term objectives at the local level, as well as the basis upon which they have sought to maintain and expand support. Beyond this, their justification for holding power also represents their long-term view of the legitimacy of Communist government in a capitalist system, and their reasons for assuming governmental power in a capitalist state.

Three elements have characterized the way that the Communists have explained their reasons for holding local power since 1925: defense of working-class interests against the state, mobilization of the working masses as an instrument of change, and concrete commitments to benefits and change at the local level. What has changed over the years has been the balance that the party has struck among these objectives, as well as the content that has given them meaning. As the Communist view of the purpose of local power has changed, their broader justification for power and the nature of their public appeal has also changed.

Prior to the Fifth Republic, the balance favored defense of working-class interests in the short run, in order to favor mobilization in the long run. 'Working-class interests' meant supporting immediate demands without regard for the fine points of bourgeois legality. The justification of local power was not in the quality or the effectiveness of day-to-day administration or even reform ('model administration'), but in the support for the day-to-day struggles of the workers.

> Municipal administration was perceived as class politics and Communist officials were expected to pursue three short-range objectives: to support the struggles of the workers, ameliorate the conditions of their lives, and maintain close links between the party and the masses.[16]

In practice, this meant that the energy of Communist elected officials was devoted to supporting strikes and demonstrations 'politically, morally and materially.' Communist-elected officials were expected to defend striking workers by using their official powers to prevent or forestall state intervention, as well as to organize political support for the objectives sought by the workers engaged in ongoing struggles. Beyond this, local mayors and councillors were urged to develop and maintain 'close contacts with the masses,' without, however, becoming 'bogged down in purely localist politics, detached from the revolutionary struggle.'[17] Communist local governments, insofar as they were able, were to provide direct benefits to 'socially disadvantaged' (i.e., workers), as opposed to those disadvantaged by their 'natural condition' (young, old and sick).

In this way, the party justified holding power in a bourgeois state as a means of protecting and developing its mass strength among the working class. Much like other local politicians, the Communists offered to protect the collective interests of their constituents against the central state, but they justified their position in local government, not in terms of local interests, but as a part of a general, coordinated and centralized revolutionary strategy.

Therefore Communist local governments went beyond simply defending workers' rights, and acted in a symbolic manner to 'challenge bourgeois legality' to establish — in practice — new political rights. Between 1925, when party mayors were first elected in the Paris region, and 1935 (the beginning of the Popular-Front period), Communist municipal governments were in continual conflict with the state. In 1925 the Communists insisted on placing women on electoral lists despite their ineligibility to hold public office. Marcel Cachin wrote in *Humanité* in 1925:

> We will present them [as candidates] in spite of the law, against the law. And thus the question of voting rights for women will be raised with new force before torpid public opinion.[18]

In this context, every vote for a woman candidate became a vote for electoral rights for women.

In subsequent years numerous Communist local officials were removed or suspended from office for supporting strikes and demonstrations (and therefore not upholding public order), and for failing to carry out administrative obligations and orders. Probing and challenging, Communist local governments pushed the limits of local independence from the central state, and emphasized their solidarity with the struggling working class. The state responded in kind. A week before the 1929 local elections the prefect of police of the Seine department ordered the mass detention of Communist militants. Throughout the pre-war period numerous local elections were annulled where Communists had won, and in March 1940, at the beginning of the Second World War, 300 Communist-dominated municipal councils were suspended.[19]

During this period, the accent was on challenge, confrontation and the defense of working-class interests. Nevertheless, and at the same time, power was justified in terms of concrete accomplishments — innovation, change and effective governments. Although party leaders warned against the dangers of establishing a 'model administration' not clearly related to the revolutionary struggle, Communist local authorities frequently claimed to have done just that. For example, in a series of articles published in *Humanité* in 1929 (reviewing the accomplishments of the first period of Communist local government) the emphasis was on new services and improved conditions. 'In Saint-Denis, despite the attacks by the bourgeois state, our municipality has accomplished a model administration.' The *Humanité* articles boasted of having transformed Villejuif from a swamp to a *cité*, of having developed hygienic facilities in Vitry, of having reduced taxes in Villetaneuse to the lowest in the Paris region.[20]

By 1935, at the end of a decade of Communist local government. *Humanité* was citing the new schools in Alfortville, Bagnolet and Villejuif, and financial order and responsibility in Gennevilliers and Gentilly as a justification for government. To the 'bluff' of the architecture of the bourgeoisie, 'we oppose the practical accomplishments of the Communist municipalities.'[21]

Thus, from the very beginning the PCF looked at local governments on two levels. On the level of long-range objectives, local government was a way-station and a means for revolutionary mobilization, while on the level of daily rhetoric and practice the actual accomplishments of local government were of greater importance. From the beginning Communist local governments strived to differentiate themselves clearly from other local governments not only by their defense of working-class action, but also by policy innovation, frequently summarized by the phrase *gestion sociale* (social administration). From the beginning they understood that their local electoral appeal was related to their accomplishments, and that policy innovation justified their holding office. In 1936, Communist Party Secretary Maurice Thorez wrote that

> Voters have for a long time seen the Communists at work. They have been able to appreciate the administrative qualities of Georges Maranne, to compare the accomplishments of our local elected officials with those of reactionary elected officials in neighboring communes. The Communists are not content to indicate remedies; they apply them.[22]

In the 1920s, Communist local governments were self-conscious innovators in the areas of services to schoolchildren (particularly summer camps), the establishment of sports programs and sports facilities (to counter the influence of church-sponsored programs), health facilities and public housing. The main lines of their commitments did not change until recently, and the links that local governments have made between requests for electoral support and their policy accomplishments has been constant over the years. However, the ideological justification has changed in some important ways. Thus, in 1925 policy objectives were 'to facilitate at the local level an easier life for the workers.' By the 1970s, the objective was 'to facilitate the union of all of the non-monopolist social groups.'[23]

For most analysts who have examined the local orientations

of the French Communist Party there are important differences between the period before the Second World War, which was characterized by a 'revolutionary orientation' and by a rigid class view of local policy, and the more recent period, which has been characterized by a desire 'to appear to be a party acceptable to a sector of public opinion larger than that of its natural partisans.'[24] In fact the ideological rhetoric did evolve towards this broader perspective, de-emphasizing challenge and confrontation, emphasizing 'democratic and social administration in the service of the whole population,' projecting the image of creative, responsive and responsible government. However, despite the evolving emphasis, the challenge and confrontation themes remain along with the others, but the functions of confrontation are seen in a somewhat different way. The function of challenge and confrontation are now seen by the party as a means of mobilization for (or against) policy goals, rather than mobilization for revolution.

> In the official discourse, struggle is the dominant element that conditions the success of great social projects. If the metro finally reaches such and such a suburban locality, if part of the highway is covered or if the path of a service road is modified, it is still the result of the struggle led by the elected officials, the party, the neighborhood or users' committees created for this objective... It is not unusual that what the party calls a struggle is after all only one very marginal element in the final decision taken by the administrative authorities, particularly when the action is limited to a petition or a series of delegations.[25]

Services, programs and new policy initiatives by the 1970s had become a way of legitimizing the national party and its program, rather than simply a means of temporarily ameliorating the conditions of an impoverished working class. Far from fearing that local government action would become 'bogged down in a purely localist politics, detached from the revolutionary struggles,' the party has come to see local government as 'a field for the most democratic experiences,' and a means of demonstrating the governmental competence of the national party.[26]

Thus, policy innovation at the local level has always been important in Communist-governed municipalities. Although actual policies have changed very little over the years, the way policy has been understood has changed in important ways. Virtually the same policy orientations have changed from embodying a tentative means for differentiating Communist local officials from others and establishing contact with the masses for other purposes, to a way of demonstrating the quality and substance of Communist government even in a bourgeois state.

In fact, the emphasis upon policy innovation and (by implication) the ability of Communist local governments to do things differently from others has created a certain number of powerful myths. For example, before the Second World War (and from time to time since) Communists frequently claimed that their social projects were paid for by a more equitable system of taxation that placed the tax burden on 'the rich.'[27] These claims have been accepted by some scholars, and have been supported by limited empirical evidence, but perhaps more important, these claims have been widely shared both by supporters and opponents of local Communism.[28] We have examined the merits of this form of 'municipal socialism' in Chapter 3, but the fact is that to the extent that they are true or false could have little to do with decisions taken by the Communist local authorities themselves. As we have pointed out, at least until 1979, local authorities could only decide the overall level of local taxes, but could not decide the levels of different tax burdens, which was a decision made by the state according to a complex administrative formula. Thus, the movement away from 'municipal socialism' noted by Tarrow is related less to the content of revenue policy than to the justification and explanation for policy.

There is evidence that the emphasis on justifying local government as an instrument of limited but important change emerged first and most strongly in pronouncements on the local rather than the national level, and therefore was less evident to scholars studying the national Communist Party. While Communist officials at the national level during the last years of the Fourth Republic were still emphasizing the priority of class defense and mobilization, literature and statements at the local level increasingly stressed the intrinsic importance of local government.[29]

As early as 1955, on the occasion of the thirtieth anniversary of Communist government in Vitry, Maurice Thorez, Party Secretary, as well as deputy from the circumscription, wrote the introduction for the special issue of the municipal bulletin. He wrote of the social and the educational programs effected by the local government as an example of what Communist government could accomplish. 'Your Communist government has changed the face of the city,' he wrote:

> The work it has accomplished during these thirty years shows what the Communists would be capable of the day that they could, following the example of their brothers of the Soviet Union and the popular democracies, reorganize the life of the nation on new foundations.[30]

Despite the references to Eastern Europe, the bulletin builds a case for Communist government based on the provision of a broad range of services, and based on the image of the local government as an active, effective policy broker with the central administration. While there are numerous references to Vitry as a working-class city, and there is considerable stress on the development of municipal services 'despite the numerous obstacles [imposed by] the government and prefectorial *tutelle*,' there is no reference whatsoever to Vitry as a defensive working-class bastion, nor is there any attempt to differentiate policy for the 'socially disadvantaged' from policy for those disadvantaged by their 'natural condition.'

Similarly, in 1962 La Seyne-sur-Mer, a working-class suburb of Toulon, celebrated the fifteenth anniversary of Communist local government. Here, too, the municipal bulletin emphasized the expansion of educational, cultural and social services as well as the importance of recent urban development. On the last page, the bulletin goes on to present additional 'reasons for the constantly growing confidence of the working class in their municipal government.' The section carefully cites the support and help that the local government gave to various strike movements over the years, and concludes by noting that 'It is normal that [workers] find among their elected officials the support that they have a right to expect in the course of conflicts in which they are opposed to their bosses.'[31]

Three years later, on the occasion of the 1965 municipal elections, the theme of working-class defense and solidarity does not appear at all in the special pre-election bulletin. Instead, the entire issue is devoted to the general benefits developed by the Communist government, with frequent unfavorable comparisons with the neighboring city of Toulon. The election statement notes with pride the success of the municipal government in securing aid from the hostile Gaullist state. The accent in this justification for Communist government is on quiet competence and accomplishment:

> A city is not administered with shouts and with gestures, with attitudes and with slogans. It is administered with work and with tenacity, with devotion and with disinterest. That is why since 1947 we have struggled to study proposals, to have them approved, to finance them and to accomplish them. Without false modesty we tell you: 'We believe we have succeeded.'[32]

By the 1970s the competence and accomplishment theme was core of the case that Communist national leaders (and local elected officials) placed before the electorate. Mobilization and working-class themes were almost entirely absent from their rhetoric. They staked their claim to local power on their ability to get things done with a strong emphasis on municipal accomplishments as an end and example in itself. Thus, the national party understood that the electoral appeal of its municipalities was:

> a tribute to the quality of administration favorable to the people, a tribute to the Communist officials in the municipalities. But we should declare above all that the time is over when the reverse is true: that the Communist ideal rallies more votes than its men, because they have not yet demonstrated their administrative capabilities. This argument is now out of date, and the Communists are properly considered those who get things done, despite the obstacles imposed by the government.[33]

Indeed, the national party argued in 1977 that voters should support PCF lists in order to obtain specific benefits.

> In communes where there is not yet an elected Communist official, you may rightly wonder: 'What do the Communists want for the commune?'... Here [are the commitments] that determine everywhere the action of the Communists, whether they are a majority or a minority in the municipal council. Here are the commitments they make, the guarantees they give you ... the construction of schools, ... sports and cultural facilities in sufficient amounts [as well as] day care centers. They consider canteens, summer camps and the most diverse social services as public services. The elderly, handicapped, women alone, families in need, always find comprehension, generous and effective aid with Communist officials.[34]

The typical local contracts proposed by Communist-led lists cite specific proposals for change and development, in addition to general criticisms of national government policies. While most of the local contracts (or manifestos) were a product of negotiations with the Socialists, the political importance of these documents is the same. They publicly tie Communist local government to policy commitments, rather than to personality or patronage networks. Moreover, the need to elaborate a program appears to create an impulsion towards active government. In response to questions about the objectives of their governments, the Communist mayors interviewed consistently referred to the priorities of the municipal contracts.

In addition to policies themselves, the Communists link the success of their governments to an open process of policy development. A high level of popular involvement is necessary, they argue, to support claims for state support. Although privately Communist local officials have sometimes questioned the efficacy of public demonstrations of support, the long-standing emphasis upon public mobilization generally distinguishes Communist local governments from others.

> The indispensable results obtained are due to the fact that they do not behave like notables or bureaucrats, far from the

> people, but that they appeal for the participation of their constituents to develop a resolute struggle in favor of the objectives for which they have been elected.[35]

Popular involvement in the development of policy is seen as necessary to support claims for state support, but above all it is the core of what they mean by local democracy. In effect, the party argues more strongly than ever that their presence at the local level should be based on their ability to deliver procedural and substantive justice.

* * *

Thus, by the late 1970s the Communist claim to local power was directly linked to claims of administrative competence and policy accomplishment — to their ability to produce collective benefits. Tarrow found that, far more than mayors from other political parties, Communist mayors tend to justify their policies in terms of the public interest. Sixty-four percent of his Communist sub-sample related their projects to the maximization of the collective interest, compared with 47 percent of the Socialists and 41 percent of the others.[36] Of course, their claims may be stronger than their actions, but the claim that power is linked to policy, and policy to the maximization of the public interest, has become the centerpiece of their claim to legitimacy. Naturally this claim also encourages voters to make their electoral judgements on what these governments *do*, rather than simply what they are and what they represent.

This way of justifying power has been an important element of Communist local government from the earliest days, and has become more important as the national party has come to see local government as a way-station to national power. The policy orientation has been one aspect of the dynamic that has generated policy initiatives by Communist governments at the local level. It is perhaps a logical consequence of the isolation of the PCF from the mainstream of national power for most of its sixty-year history that it should aspire to broaden the constraints on local initiative and local policy-making.

Notes

1. See the summary of this argument in Mark Kesselman, 'Research Perspective in Comparative Local Politics,' in Terry Clark, ed., *Comparative Community Politics* (Beverly Hills: Sage, 1974), pp. 364–7; the argument has been made most persuasively by Jean-Pierre Worms, 'Le Préfet et ses notables,' *Sociologie du Travail*, July 1966; it has been used most recently by Peter Gourevitch in *Paris and the Provinces* (Berkeley: University of California Press, 1980).
2. See Jeanne Becquart-Leclerq, *Paradoxes du pouvoir local* (Paris: Presses de la FNSP, 1976), pp. 205–6.
3. Marcel Rosette, *La Gestion communale dans l'action* (Paris: Éditions Sociales, 1977).
4. Henry Canacos, *A l'Écoute des villes de France*, cited in Raymond Pronier, *Les Municipalités communistes* (Paris: Ballard, 1983), p. 209.
5. Becquart-Leclerq, op. cit., p. 205.
6. Ibid., pp. 160–2.
7. Sidney Tarrow, *Between Center and Periphery* (New Haven: Yale University Press, 1977), p. 169; and 'Party Activists in Public Office,' in Donald Blackmer and Sidney Tarrow, *Communism in Italy and France* (Princeton: Princeton University Press, 1975), p. 163.
8. Ezra N. Suleiman, *Politics, Power and Bureaucracy in France* (Princeton: Princeton University Press, 1974), p. 363.
9. Ibid., p. 365.
10. Ibid., p. 366.
11. Jean Montaldo, *La France communiste* (Paris: Albin Michel, 1978), p. 159.
12. Ibid., p. 160.
13. *Le Grand Ensemble*, unpublished report, Vitry, 1974.
14. Tarrow, *Between Center and Periphery*, pp. 103–6. However, there is evidence that, at least in the Paris region, the distribution of state-provided services favors municipalities governed by the right. Preteceille found the highest levels of state and private facilities in right-wing cities, and the highest level of municipal (and the lowest level of private) facilities in Communist governed cities. See 'Left-wing Local Governments and Services Policy in France,' *International Journal of Urban and Regional Research*, 5, No. 3, 1981, pp. 418–19.
15. Ibid., p. 168.
16. Jerome Milch, 'The PCF and Local Government: Continuity and Change,' in Blackmer and Tarrow, op. cit., p. 345.
17. Jacques Duclos, 'Programme municipal du Parti Communiste en 1935' (Paris, n.d.), quoted in Milch, ibid., p. 346.
18. *Humanité*, March 7, 1925, quoted in Pronier, op.cit., p. 23.
19. Françqis Platone, 'L'Implantation du parti communiste francais dans la Seine et sa conception de l'administration communale,' (mémoire, diplôme supérieure d'études et de recherche politique, Paris, FNSP, 1967).
20. *Humanité*, April 24, 26, 29, 30, May 5, cited in Pronier, op. cit., pp. 26–7.

21. Ibid.
22. Maurice Thorez, *Fils du peuple* (Paris: Éditions Sociales, 1960), cited by Pronier, op. cit., p. 216.
23. Pronier, op. cit., pp. 216–18.
24. Ibid., pp. 216–17; also see Milch, op. cit., p. 347, and Tarrow, *Between Center and Periphery*, p. 167.
25. Pronier, op. cit., p. 211.
26. Milch, op. cit., p. 347.
27. See, for example, the review of *Humanité* in 1936 cited by Pronier, especially *Humanité*, April 12, 1936.
28. Tarrow, for example, accepts these claims at face value, while Thibaud and Montaldo have found limited evidence to support them: Tarrow, op. cit., p. 167; Paul Thibaud, 'Le Communisme municipal,' *Esprit*, October 1967, p. 415; Montaldo, *Les Finances du PCF* (Paris: Albin Michel, 1977), pp. 14–18.
29. Jacques Duclos, 'Les Municipalités au service des masses laborieuses,' Report to the Fourteenth Congress of the PCF, 1956, p. 107, cited in Ronald Tiersky, *French Communism 1920–1972* (New York: Columbia University Press, 1974), p. 352.
30. *Bulletin Municipal de Vitry-sur-Seine*, December 1955, p. 1.
31. *Bulletin Municipal de la Seyne-sur-Mer*, December 1962.
32. Ibid., February, 1965, p. 1.
33. Jean Gacon, 'Géographie et sociologie électorale du PCF,' *Cahier de l'Institut Maurice Thorez*, January–February 1973, p. 23.
34. Rosette, op. cit., pp. 297–302.
35. Ibid., pp. 9–10.
36. Cited by Milch, op. cit., p. 353.

5 Explaining Policy: Structure and Process

The structure and process of local government in cities governed by Communists have always been different from that of other cities, primarily because of the strong links to a national party. National PCF links have been important in the evolution and in the structuring of support for Communists at the local level, and they have been an important element in the development of a justification for local government power. (See Chapters 2 and 4.) In these ways, we have argued, the national party connection has had a strong influence on policy initiation and innovation.

In this chapter we will analyze the impact of the mixture of control and complex linkage provided by the party on the policy-making process at the local level, as well as the role of popular-front alliances, and local political forces, in the structure and process of policy formation. The national party connection, the alliance with the Socialists and relations with local groups, each in different ways has stimulated, defined and ordered local policy-planning and policy-making. To some extent this has been the direct result of commitments made by the national party that were analyzed in the last chapter. However, new projects and new services have also been the result of a competitive policy process that has been generated by the more complex structure in Communist-governed municipalities. With limited capacity to gain benefits from the central state, the competitive process has strengthened the will of these governments to initiate policy demands.

The role of the party

The relationship between local Communist governments and the national party has been frequently marked by tension, and, from time to time, open conflict. Clearly the ability of the party to maintain discipline among its local officials has been limited, and voter loyalty to the party has sometimes been weak. Three mayors in the Paris region left the party in 1930–1, without losing their positions in by-elections that followed. Between 1930 and 1940, every mayor of Saint-Denis was a 'renegade,' although five of these six mayors had, with party support, defeated a previous renegade.

As a result of the problems encountered during the 1930s, the party has been particularly careful to distance local officials from decision-making positions within the party organization. However, the tension between conflicting perspectives of local elected officials and the party organization has continued to be an important element of Communist local government, particularly during periods when the national party line is changing or unclear. For example, at the 1956 PCF Congress, Jacques Duclos delivered a major report on the municipalities, in which he commented that 'in the course of recent years, a certain climate of irresponsibility has been created in the administration of the activities of Communist municipalities.'[1]

In recent years, the normal tension has perhaps been accentuated by the expansion of united left coalitions at the local level after 1965, and then the collapse of the united left at the national level in 1977. The national party has attempted to develop some degree of control over the imposition of national political positions at the local level as well as local policy priorities, but it has probably achieved more success in the former objective than the latter. In its own journals party spokesmen have continued to complain about the difficulties in imposing controls over localities:

> Basically, what really happens is the opposite of what the reactionaries say; we have developed no strategy for the colonization of the municipalities, but we have sometimes forgotten the proper role of the Communist Party. So that, at the limit, it is the Communist Party that runs the risk of being absorbed, colonized by municipal activity, and not the reverse.[2]

The national party has, over the years, established channels — both formal and informal — for transmitting its propaganda campaigns down to the local level and publicizing in the communes the essential themes of party discourse. While some of these themes require action, the action is generally symbolic.[3] However, there has been considerable resistance to implementing some of the more controversial national lines during the past few years. The anti-immigrant campaign, initiated by some Communist-governed municipalities in the later 1970s, was staunchly resisted by others when it became the national line during the presidential campaign in 1981.[4] In the end, only a handful of municipalities took up the campaign, while the others remained silent. (See Chapter 3.) Resistance to the party line is difficult to control in part because local Communist officials are frequently popular 'notables' with a local following that is not easily dissuaded by party condemnation. The case of Roger Fajnzylberg, the former mayor of Sèvres, is an interesting case in point.

Fajnzylberg, whose entire career had been as a functionary of the party, was the very popular mayor of Sèvres until 1983. In this upper-middle class town, Fajnzylberg had established a solid 'administrative' reputation as a man who could get things done. Indeed, in 1981, the leader of the RPR in Sèvres had remarked that

> We should not confuse the problem. Our mayor does not impose his ideology. He does his duty as an elected official well, and for that deserves our respect ... I know that if I criticize the mayor without coherent grounds, all true Sèvriens would fall all over me and say: 'You've lost your head.'[5]

In October 1981, he was excluded from his party functions without being formally expelled for having participated in a dissident journal launched by Henri Fiszbin. Although the committee of the party section (of which he was a member) refused to meet with him present, the members of the Sèvres municipal council (Communists and Socialists) 'reaffirmed their confidence' in the mayor, 'our comrade and friend.' Under the circumstances, the local PCF section decided not to attempt to force new local elections before 1983.[6] In the first round of the 1983 local elections, the Communists proposed their own list, while Fajnzylberg headed the official Socialist list.

Fajnzylberg was able to rally considerable Communist support, even among militants.[7] His support among the electorate was more impressive. Although his list lost (by just over 100 votes — 1 percent), the official PCF list was able to attract only 628 votes — 6 percent — on the first ballot. Fajnzylberg complained that the second ballot loss was due to a secret party directive to oppose his list, although, with some embarrassment, the party officially supported the Fajnzylberg list.[8]

This case provides us with a sense of the limits of party control, even when a local elected official has directly challenged the national party line. While to varying degrees the political directives of the national party are followed by local elected officials, actions implied by these directives are less apt to be followed. Where actions on issues remote from the commune call for mass participation, their success is most conditional and most questionable. Thus, few of the voters in Sèvres were willing to support the orthodox Communist list in 1983, few municipal governments were willing or able to mobilize in the anti-immigrant campaign in 1980–1, and clearly few Communist voters were willing to follow a putative secret directive to vote against Mitterrand in the second round of the presidential elections in 1981.[9] The ultimate recourse to discipline and expulsion has always been costly to the party, and therefore is generally avoided except in cases of open and public dissidence.[10]

On the level of local policy-making, party control is less effective, and seems to be less sought in a consistent way. The PCF Central Committee adopted a resolution in June 1977, specifying that local Communist officials should 'experiment with new forms of democratic administration, flexible and close to the population,' without having to worry about any 'meddling control' by the party organization.[11] In fact, the separation between the role of elected official and party militant seems to be clearer among Communist local officials than among their Socialist counterparts.[12] Although various party committees have developed projects for local government, these projects have had only a limited impact on policy initiation, and have depended upon local conditions and the authority of individual mayors.

We have found no evidence, moreover, that party links provide an important conduit for accomplishing local policy objectives, and our interviews consistently support Tarrow's report that Communist mayors generally use administrative channels for policy bargaining.[13] When we asked a sample of new Communist mayors in 1978 about their most important contacts for advancing their most important projects, we received two kinds of answers, depending on the prior and/or current political experience of the mayor. Those mayors who were not, or had not been, deputies claimed that their most important contacts were with the departmental prefecture or the local subprefect, while some claimed that for some projects they were helped by neighboring local officials from parties of the left.

Other mayors, however, exuded the confidence of well-established political notables. Claude Lamblin, the mayor of Reims and general councillor for the Marne, claimed good relations with elected officials from all parties, and travelled frequently to Paris to lobby for grants and loans, and to attract industry to Reims. The mayor of Antony, Aubry, claimed a wide range of important contacts as a result of his position as a senator, and argued that his intervention at the ministerial level was important for freeing funds allocated at the department level. Similarly, Bourdu, the mayor of Chelles, stressed the importance of his wide-ranging political connections and his ability to intervene directly at the ministerial level. Bourdu had been a deputy and was also a general councillor for the Marne. He made a point of contrasting his position with that of other Communist-governed municipalities that did not benefit from a well-placed mayor. Finally, Tricart, the mayor of Poissy, who was both a former deputy and a member of the financial control commission of the central committee of the PCF, argued that he used limited political contacts with mayors from all political parties in the department, and his extensive administrative and political contacts in Paris to advance the interests of the commune.

Experience with higher elected office did not automatically endow a Communist mayor with the confidence of his contacts, however. The Mayor of Villeneuve-Saint-Georges,

Gaudon, had been a senator for ten years, but the experience had left him embittered about his relations with elected officials of the right. He claimed no direct political or administrative contacts with Paris ('I do not believe them to be effective'), argued that cooperation with elected officials of the right was generally not possible, and implied that Aubry's (Antony) direct intervention was unique. Gaudon was the only Communist mayor that I interviewed who claimed that his 'initiatives were systematically badly received' by the administration because he was a Communist.

Thus, there is considerable variation among Communist mayors in the way they have used and developed their contacts. However, not a single mayor, regardless of his position within the party and whatever his political position or experience, claimed that the party played an important role in helping him to secure his local policy objectives. This does not mean that the party is a mere shadow, or is unimportant in local politics. The party has maintained a dominant role in the selection of candidates for the position of mayor, especially in the larger towns, and it has maintained and developed a network of channels and contacts that are important in the development of policy initiatives at the local level.

In contrast to mayors of all other parties, Communist mayors are selected by their party, and, particularly in the larger towns, it is experience within the party that qualifies a candidate.[14] Almost all of the mayors who won their posts in 1977 had become members of the PCF either during the period immediately after the Second World War, or during the early years of the Fifth Republic; all of the mayors interviewed for this study had been party functionaries (generally at the federation — department — level) prior to running for mayor. In general, it appears that in recent years it is the confederal committees of the department federations that are responsible for naming candidates for mayor for the most important communes in the department. The result is what Pronier refers to as something approaching 'self-designation.'[15] Nevertheless, some designations have been made of popular party militants with limited experience in the organization, such as Claude Lamblin, the mayor of Reims, who had been a militant and local section secretary only five years before he was designated a candidate in the cantonal elections in 1976. One year after he won and entered the general council of the Marne, he was named to head the Union of the Left list for Reims in 1977.

In smaller towns, local sections take more responsibility for finding and designating candidates, but there are sometimes conflicts for the nomination among local sections. In 1977, in the Oise department, two local Communist sections — one based in the town, the other in the large enterprise of Pechiney-Ugine-Kuhlmann — competed for the acceptance of their candidate to head the Union of the Left list for the town of Villers-Saint-Paul. The federation designated the candidate supported by the town-based organization, but militants from the two sections were apparently selected to fill out the list. Nevertheless, the rivalry remained intense, even after the Communist-led list was victorious, and the rivalry was intensified by a growing antagonism towards the new mayor that resulted a year later in the mass resignation of all of the Communist (and Socialist) members of the town council.[16]

Control by the party department federations over candidate designation at the local level provides an important, if not always successful filter for promoting the kinds of candidates that suit the changing party line. It also facilitates the manipulation and distribution of elected offices (*saupoudrage des mandats*) among Communist militants that reduces the possibilities of the development of independent personal fiefs over time.[17] At any given moment, Communist mayors of larger cities tend to accumulate mandates at about the same rate as mayors of other parties. However, specific accumulations tend not to endure; after a short period of time Communist mayors generally surrender one or more of the elected posts that they have won. Thus, the party has been reasonably effective in preventing the accumulation of elective offices from becoming a means of advancement within the party. Clearly, the party controls the advancement of political office-holders, and not vice versa.

The party has also established linkage between national priorities and local politics through a national network of direct contacts among mayors that has developed over the years. Direct contacts among Communist local officials have existed since the 1920s. Before the Second World War all Communist mayors in the Paris region belonged to the Union of Communist Cities, as well as to the Association of Mayors of the Seine (department). The union focused mainly on technical aid to Communist-governed cities, but also elaborated a municipal program for each of the pre-war local elections.

In 1947, the PCF created an Association of Republican Elected Officials as a forum for maintaining and developing contacts with other local officials of the left. The association was transformed into the larger FNER (Fédération Nationale des Élus Republicains) in 1964 — a prelude to the effort to develop a common program. In 1949 the association began to publish *Information municipale*, a monthly devoted primarily to an exchange of information on technical matters and a limited number of political articles. The FNER remained the organized forum of contact for Communist local elected officials until 1977, when the PCF, for the first time, organized its own association of local elected officials.

In the early 1970s, with the expansion of its presence at the local level, the Communist Party had begun to modify and reinforce the structure through which it attempted to coordinate and influence policy at the local level. Rather than rely upon the regular party organization or the contacts within the FNER, the central committee began to establish its own direct contact among mayors and municipal councillors.

During the spring of 1972, the central committee organized a general meeting of Communist mayors and other elected office-holders for the first time.[18] A year later, the effort was formalized when the party refurbished an existing quarterly journal with a new format (*Bulletin de l'Élu Communiste*), 'not only as a source of information and a bulletin where party responsibles write, but also [as a] place for the exchange of experience and points of view of Communist elected officials.'[19] At the same time the central committee re-established the (pre-war) Central Commission for Municipal Policy to coordinate policy.

In February 1978, the quarterly was transformed into a monthly — *l'Élu d'Aujourd'hui* — to serve as the official publication of the ANECR (Association Nationale des Élus Communistes et Républicains) that had been launched nine months earlier. Although local office-holders continued to belong to the FNER, the party clearly emphasized the new organization as the focus of its attention. Both the new publication and the association, which had been gradually organized in each department, represented a considerable effort by the party both to encourage direct contact among Communist mayors and municipal councillors and to train and socialize the large influx of new elected officials whose numbers had doubled after the 1977 municipal elections.

> Thousands of new municipal councillors, confronted from one day to the next with complex problems of administration, needed information and exchanges of experience in quantity [and] quality, and with rapidity.[20]

In developing this new structure, the party both increased the density of contacts among its local elected officials and exerted more intense central control over them. Perhaps fearful that the mayors would become an independent force within the party, the central bureaucracy quickly took control of the key positions of ANECR. Both the secretariat and the monthly publication were quickly dominated by the central committee's commission.[21]

L'Élu d'Aujourd'hui is filled with articles that deal with the daily administration ofa middle-sized city in France, but the emphasis of each issue between 1978 and 1981 was on those issues of particular concern to the PCF: the differences between Communist- and Socialist-governed municipalities, the weight of the obligations imposed by the central state and, by 1981, the problems of security and immigration. The complex role of coordination is indicated by the statement by Marcel Rosette in June, 1978:

> The role of the association: It is therefore by making democracy our daily political practice that we are going to move forward. In order to better arrive there, Communist office-holders will find in the life of their party the rich *experience* of an avant-garde party. Attached to the principle of *democratic centralism*, they will contribute the perfection of its functioning, to reinforce it . . . because the Communist Party does not confuse the activity of political parties and that of governing authorities, Communist elected officials consider that their *primary task* is to fulfil with care the mandate that they have received from the population. It is precisely to permit these office-holders to accomplish their specific tasks better that the central Committee has decided

> ... on the establishment of the Association of Communist and Republican office-holders. The order of the day is to devote all efforts to the departmental associations, to better inform office-holders, coordinate their activities, exchange their experiences; they must be the object of permanent attention by the federal [departmental] directors of the party.[22]

Rosette's statement betrays an interesting mix of a desire for both coordination of experience and party direction.

Nevertheless, despite these heroic efforts by the party, it is not clear that political coordination was any more effective after 1978 than before. Certainly one result of this structural coordination has been a limited range of coordinated policy innovations. Central committee resolutions in 1966, for example, resulted in the establishment of a multitude of cultural programs in Communist-governed municipalities, ranging from municipal cultural commissions to state subsidized *centres d'animation culturaux* and the larger *maisons de la culture*.[23] By 1981, such programs were generally thought of as programs of the left and of Communist-governed cities in particular, although much of the impetus for local cultural services had come from the attempts of the ministry of culture under André Malraux to decentralize culture by providing state subsidies. In fact most of the larger local cultural programs were in cities governed by the left.

However, the PCF has always been ambivalent about its support for local culture. The party has tended to view 'culture' broadly as including sports, education, science and technology. 'The field of culture, including the whole of social, professional, familial and individual life, ... must respond to the needs of the evolution of science, of technology, of professional, social and civic life.'[24] This general view has frequently placed central party policy in conflict with the activities of those hired by local governments to run their cultural programs.[25] Therefore, pressure from the party stimulated the launching of cultural programs in the 1960s, while the ambivalence of the party towards high culture has from time to time been responsible for local conflict.

> It is interesting to note that, despite a decision of the controlling minister, Gaston Deferre, permitting the

> titularization of socio-cultural promoters, a larger number of Communist mayors has greatly limited the [number of] nominations. In effect, there is great fear of no longer being able to exercise any pressure on these personnel.[26]

Central party priorities also seem to have influenced the establishment of other services over the years. After 1970, the party emphasized the need to upgrade and expand local information systems, and in the early 1970s Communist municipalities began to cooperate in the use of computers. In 1975, the party stressed the need for youth services (and *maisons de la jeunesse*), and more recently the need for immigration and economic services. In each case the party priority, publicly stated, was reflected in local priorities, but not universally. Thus, in a survey of commune services (1979–80) conducted by the National Institute of Statistical and Economic Studies, several Communist cities are among the few lacking *maisons de la jeunesse*.[27]

Party coordination means that policy decisions are considered in an arena that is larger than the municipality. The party structure at the federation level for some time has provided an arena within which Communist local officials have made contact, discussed problems and compared accomplishments. Jean-Pierre Hoss, in his study of the Paris suburbs of Argenteuil and Bézons during the mid-1960s, observed that these kinds of contacts between the two mayors were frequently marked by policy competition.

> The objective of these contacts is to confront the problems of the two cities, to study possible solutions, but above all, to harmonize municipal policies . . . so that one commune is not further ahead — or behind — the other with regard to accomplishments. Whatever is undertaken in Bézons must be [undertaken] in Argenteuil, and vice versa.[28]

Competition on policy was also evident among local Communist officials first elected in 1977 whom I interviewed in 1978 and 1980. Their point of departure for policy initiatives was not only what the previous governments of the right had done, but also the successes and the failures of the more established Communist local governments. Thus, the mayor of

Antony and his assistants referred frequently (if somewhat sympathetically) to the failures of Vitry in urban planning, and the mayors of several of the (then) newly-won municipalities contrasted the open process of policy-development in their towns with the ossification of the old bastions. One key municipal official, who had formerly served in Vitry, saw the experiment in Antony as a reaction to the failures of Vitry, while the mayor of Houilles argued that the notion of a bastion was 'dead,' that such a 'closed' community no longer corresponded to political realities, and that Communist-governed cities like Houilles were in fact the wave of the future. On the other hand, while the older bastions were sometimes criticized (quite openly) for their poor urban planning and closed political processes, it was clear that the new Communist-governed municipalites accepted that their model of activist government that must provide a range of social services.

In addition to directives, advice and an arena of coordination, the party has also provided a network of service organizations for its municipalities. From summer camp services to studies for housing and urban development and computer services, firms associated indirectly with the party have long provided such services. Although these firms have been frequently referred to as a means through which the party ultimately derives considerable income, they also provide alternatives to the state administration for services and advice.[29] They contribute to the relative autonomy of Communist-governed municipalities *vis-à-vis* the state, but also augment the greater uniformity of policies and planning among these municipalities, as well as their greater dependency upon the Communist party.[30]

None of these firms is officially owned or controlled by the party, but their existence and their functions are well known, *L'Élu d'Aujourd'hui* is filled with their publicity, and stories about new developments, initiatives and services constantly refer to the same firms.[31] Like interchanges of information and accomplishments, the use of party-associated firms feeds both policy competition as well as uniformity. There are several cases that indicate that the use of the same service organizations often produces the same policy choices, or at least similar ways of doing things. Thus, during the 1970s, similar (and connected) systems for computer data collection and analysis were nstalled in a large number of Communist-governed munici-)alities by a company associated with the Communist Party SOGIR).[32] In 1982 Sigma-formation, also associated with the)arty, produced virtually the same programs for training and)reparing young people for entrance into the labor market in ıbout forty Communist-governed communes in the Paris 'egion, although each program was supposed to be tailored to he specific needs of each commune.[33]

However, differences in policy among Communist-governed nunicipalities in important areas that have been cited in this :hapter and in Chapter 3 indicate that service organizations nay be more important as a tool for municipal policy levelopment than as a tool for party control. As a tool for)olicy development, party service organizations feed both)olicy competition as well as uniformity. They also augment he bargaining power of Communist mayors *vis-à-vis* the state. The director of the section of the ministry of equipment in :harge of urban planning (the GEP) for the new town of Évry n the Paris region contended that the technical services ıssociated with the PCF that worked with the Communist mayors invariably made his work of coordination more lifficult by making it easier for mayors to redefine problems in echnical terms. Moreover, the very fact that Communist mayors have a choice of technical services has meant that they :an more effectively manipulate rivalries within the state ıdministration (see the examples of Arles and Vitry cited in Chapter 4).

The most important effect of the party's efforts to increase :entral coordination has been to increase contacts among Communist local office-holders, and such contacts have served as a stimulus for policy development. Party coordination has also encouraged Communist mayors to think of their communes as active initiators of new policies, and to think in similar ways about policy alternatives at the local level. Mayors strenuously denied that the local party section had any supervisory role in policy-making, but they readily admitted the connection between national and local priorities, at least in a general way. With the development of a national contract in 1971 and 1977, the national line on general objectives and priorities became clearer, and — seemingly — a more powerful stimulus.

Nevertheless, there are certainly differences in substance, style and process among Communist-governed cities, differences that are sometimes related to demography and tax structure. Thus, Antony and Athis-Mons, with relatively small working-class populations, have placed more emphasis on balanced urban development (with a smaller number of housing units) than have Vitry and Chelles, which have a larger number of demands for housing. Chelles and Antony, which have a small industrial base and therefore rely heavily on regressive local property taxes for their income, depend more heavily than other Communist-governed cities on fees for service, rather than tax revenues, to finance their municipal operations. After the 1977 election, the new municipal council in Chelles decided to reorganize the city bus service, and to charge sliding-scale fees. Until 1977, the service had been free. A number of Communist and Socialist local officials that I interviewed also insisted that there was an important difference in style and process between the older Communist bastions and the cities with newly-elected Communist and *union-de-gauche* governments. The newer governments, they insisted, were more open, more pragmatic, less bureaucratic, and better organized than the older ones.

The role of party competition

The Communist Party link has also stimulated policy innovation and development in an indirect way, through the unity of the left strategy with the Socialist Party. The most important result of this strategy from the point of view of this study has been the restructuring of political life at the local level. (See Chapter 2.) By 1977, in all but a few of the 221 towns with more than 30,000 population, the Communists and Socialists presented united lists in fulfillment of their national agreement. However, the result in the 141 towns where the two parties governed together between 1977 and 1981 was not unity, but a cooperative/competitive relationship that defined the politics and the policies of these municipalities. Where the balance of forces was close, as it was in many of these towns, competition was particularly intense.

For most of the seventy-two municipalities with Communist

mayors between 1977 and 1983, cooperation between the two party groups was defined by a local contract negotiated during the preparation of the 1977 municipal elections. There remained, however, many areas of competition about the details of agreements, disagreements on the hiring of municipal personnel, and innumerable disagreements about process and consultation. In fact, within the cooperative framework of the municipal contract, both party groups were engaged in intense inter-party competition, with each party attempting to outbid the other in order to build political support, and the tools of competition were policy and patronage.

In contrast to municipalities governed by the right, party group competition in cities governed by the left is highly structured, and it defines the main lines of the decision-making process. Where the balance of forces is close, policy tends to emerge from bargaining between group leaders in the municipal bureau, generally reducing the role of the bureaucratic services, and politicizing the entire process through the committees of the municipal council (the *commissions municipales*). Competition and opposition have been a relatively rare phenomenon in all French municipalities, even in the larger ones, and, in general, decision-making power tends to be concentrated in the hands of the mayor who sometimes collaborates with deputy (assistant) mayors.[34] There is evidence from towns that elected new Communist mayors in 1977 that while former mayors of the center-right had given a relatively free administrative hand to civil service heads in particular departments, the new *union-de-gauche* governments forced the civil service to the periphery of the political process.

For example, in Poissy, where the balance between the Communists and Socialists was roughly equal after 1977, a dozen committees of municipal councillors were formed after the 1977 elections. Policy initiative quickly shifted from civil service department chiefs to the committees, and decision-making from civil service collaboration with the mayor, to collaboration between party groups in the municipal bureau and party representatives on the municipal commissions. Conflicts over the important policies divided along party lines. (The two most important conflicts during the first year involved Communist support for free textbooks for both public and Catholic school children and the choice of a summer camp for local children. In 1977, the council chose a Communist camp by one vote, but in 1978 they agreed to use both a Communist and a Socialist camp.) In a competitive political environment the scope of involvement of elected officials increased, leaving little room for civil service initiative.

In Communist-governed cities Socialist groups have given a great deal of attention to maintaining the depth of involvement of municipal councillors. In Athis-Mons, the head of the Socialist group emphasized the importance of the work of the resuscitated council committees both for socialist input and more general policy development. In Chelles, the head of the Socialist group cited the lack of coordinated work between the municipal bureau and the municipal commissions as a major source of disagreement with the mayor. In protest over this procedural gap, the Socialist groups refused to vote for the municipal budget in 1977. (Coordination with the committees was reinforced in the discussions of the supplementary budget.)[35]

In general, party competition in *union-de-gauche* municipalities both intensified and complicated the policy-making process. In Antony and in Athis-Mons party groups agreed that the existing urban development plan was not satisfactory, and they joined in pressuring the administration for revision. (See Chapter 3.) However, they intensely disagreed on an acceptable plan for over a year. Given the intensity of competition between the two parties, policy debate is not easily contained within the limited arena of the municipal bureau, and there appears to be a tendency for the weaker party to expand the arena of conflict, and therefore expand the range of options being considered. In Communist-governed municipalities this has been achieved through real and symbolic public acts, such as Socialists refusing to vote for the annual municipal budget, or, as in the case of the debate over urban renewal in Antony, by leaking to the public a confidential report on an urban renewal plan prepared by a *bureau d'études* close to the Communist Party. Conflicts between Communist and Socialist groups at the local level have been given widespread publicity, usually as a demonstration of growing tensions between the two national parties after 1977, but in almost every case (and there have been antagonists on both sides), the source of the tension is local competition for policy or position.

However, there have been clear limits to local conflict. Between 1977 and 1983, despite the breakup of the national alliance, there were few corresponding breakups of local coalitions. The reasons for limited reverberations were alluded to frequently by local officials of both parties, who, in contrast to national party officials tended to stress the specific local issues rather than more general party antagonism.[36]

For most of the Socialists and Communists collaborating at the local level, their coalitions have been an arena for a continuing but limited intra-party and inter-party struggle. Communist local officials must maintain Socialist local support in order to maintain the vast majority of their local government strongholds. In general, this objective was more important for them than the national party objective to halt and roll back the growing Socialist ascendancy within the left after 1977, and it provided an outside limit for local political conflict. Indeed, the June 1977 resolution of the central committee of the PCF seems to have facilitated this priority by separating party and local government roles. (See above, p. 112.) Interviews with both Communist and Socialist officials in 1978 and 1981 confirmed that where there is a balance of forces between the two groups, limits are carefully observed and there was an effective 'conflictual collaboration' after 1977. Communist mayors frequently expressed both a strong attachment to local government, as well as optimism about local policy achievements:

> I love responsibilities, and to be mayor is the most difficult of all. [A mayor] must be an urban planner, a good administrator and possess extraordinary human qualities . . . Our objective is not to change society, but to deal with concrete daily problems. It is better for the workers to have a Communist mayor. We can change things in daily life. Half of those who come to see me want jobs, and I cannot do much. But I can initiate a new hospital, help those most in need of help, make choices to serve the greatest number.[37]

Socialists in cities with Communist mayors stressed strong and continuing links with their local party organizations. Indeed, their purpose in participating in local government, they frequently argued, was to build new party strength. In this sense, they were consistently more militant than their Communist colleagues; their commitments were more national than local. The deputy mayor of Sevran emphasized that local responsibilities were important, but: 'I am not kidding myself. It is fine to be a deputy mayor but what is really important is to build the Socialist Party. Above all I am a militant.'

In fact, building the party at the local level relates to the struggle within the Socialist Party, since most of these officials who agreed to participate in coalition governments with the Communists displaced Socialist groups that were committed to third force coalitions (with centrist parties). 'That is what differentiates us from the old group. They forgot that they were socialists.'

For the Socialists, limits were imposed by necessity. The Socialist deputy mayor of Chelles argues that the relationship between the local groups of Socialist elected officials and the national Socialist Party was very strong but if a complete break in the *union-de-gauche* strategy would occur, the local group would probably break apart. Limits were also imposed by a certain level of respect for their Communist colleagues. Socialist officials were careful to emphasize that their disagreements were political but not personal. As the deputy mayor of Sevran commented:

> I am anti-communist to the core. I work with them well on this level, and I respect them because they are supported by the working class. They are fine militants here, and if there were no PCF apparatus, they would be fine socialist militants . . .

On balance, conflict between the two parties at the municipal level has been limited and contained, and has stimulated policy development by broadening policy options being considered. Because conflict has also reflected the attempt by elected officials of both parties to maintain access to policy-making and positions of influence, it has also served to broaden political participation. The decision-making process tends to be one of bargaining between group leaders in the municipal bureau, but, because there is competitive party government, party groups frequently attempt to outbid one another in policy terms in order to build support.

The role of groups and associations

Even where party competition is less intense, however, policy activism is often stimulated by the process through which Communist-governed municipalities tend to mobilize support for the objectives they seek from the state. Far more than their counterparts in the United States, French mayors have roots in large number of local associations. Socialist and Communist mayors have served frequently as militants in the CGT (Communists) or the Federation of National Education (Socialist), as well as numerous other associations that are linked with each party.[38] If in municipalities governed by the right, these associations generally serve as '... a network of clientelist links that assure re-election,' in Communist-governed municipalities, associations are integrated into a process of political mobilization and decision-making.

From the earliest years of Communist local government, the party expended great energy in developing a network of 'mass organizations' at the local level, organizations associated with the party, but that included many non-Communist members. Indeed, this was the core of the 'counter-society' that the PCF tried to build over the years. However, by the 1970s, most of the mass organizations specifically associated with the party had lost their vitality.[39] Nevertheless, the party and local governments have continued to emphasize the importance of links to a wide range of local organizations, which they now refer to as 'local associations,' rather than 'mass organizations.' 'We attach great interest to the development of association life ... There are great possibilities for effective coordination in them,' argues the party handbook on local government. Of course associations or committees cannot assume the decision-making or the administrative role of the municipal council, and local power cannot be parceled out. Nevertheless, 'Their participation in the elaboration of a project, their contribution to some actions, is perfectly related to our permanent concern for responding to the needs of the population.'[40] Moreover, Communist local governments have developed a broad view of *la vie associative*, and have stressed relations with politically and socially diverse groups. 'The commune, like French society, is characterized by social, political and ideological diversity of its population. All democratic administration presumes that this diversity is taken into account.'[41]

Communist mayors take pride in their ability to use popular mobilization as a means of openly confronting the state and gaining benefits they would not otherwise obtain 'because they effectively organize this battle [for state benefits] with the population and because they emphasize the support of the population.'[42]

Interviews and observations confirm Hoss's analysis that there has been a conscious attempt to integrate associations into the development of policy, and to use mobilized groups to generate support from the state.[43] Indeed, Communist local governments carry this process one step further by mobilizing 'latent groups,' such as the elderly, the young or those who use public transportation.

> With more knowledge and diligence than 'bourgeois' municipalities, local Communist leaders activate interest groups which until then were poorly equipped or incapable of organizing themselves and lacked a feeling of solidarity. In these situations the Communist team becomes the political actor by which 'the latent group' comes into existence and through which certain claims may be satisfied.[44]

Neighborhood committees, linked to deliberations of 'extended commissions' of the municipal council, frequently serve as arenas of mobilization for local policy priorities. 'We want the crèche that you need,' the mayor of Antony told the author he explained to a neighborhood committee. 'Help us to secure the credits from the state.'

The dominant relationship between Communist-governed municipalities and the administration is careful bargaining and negotiations, but 'appeals to the population, and the recourse to struggle' in the context of bargaining is frequently important.[45] Thus, in the internal report on housing development in Vitry, the Communist municipal authorities credit a 1962 compromise with state representatives that increased the number of low-income apartments in the development area to 'an important success gained on the basis of a battle led with the aid of the population and of the deputy.' In elaborating their strategy to further modify the plan in 1974 (this time to get state subsidies for more park areas and services), the municipal authorities outline a broad campaign that combines both the intervention of the deputy and general councillors, as well as 'information, consultation and the action of the population . . .' Mobilization is taken seriously by Communist local officials as a tool in their interactions with the state, and as a means of developing and maintaining support.

There are some indications, however, that links with associations are more than simple transmission belts for popular mobilization. In general, both Communist and Socialist local officials agree that contact with organized groups takes place after the essential decisions are reached in the municipal bureau. The mayor of Poissy emphasized the need 'to avoid anarchy,' and no mayor or assistant mayor interviewed credited a local association with originating any policy departure. Nevertheless, in municipalities governed by the left, particularly in those governed by Communist mayors, numerous local associations are integrated into the policy-making process. The changes in municipal organization cited most frequently by Communist local officials (as well as by Socialists in towns with Communist mayors) that were elected in 1977, are the expanded network of *commissions municipales* and the links between these *commissions* and local associations.

The open connection between *commissions municipales* and local associations was first accomplished successfully in the Communist-governed town of Sarcelles after 1965, where 240 representatives of local associations worked regularly with thirty-five municipal councillors in thirteen municipal commissions. Although the Sarcelles experiment did not become widespread, more limited forms of regular contact have become part of the normal process of government in most Communist-governed municipalities.

These contacts themselves seem to create a certain pressure for broad policy development. Hoss, for example, found that in Argenteuil policy demands were transmitted from associations and neighborhood committees, through the extended commissions, to the municipal council.[46] By 'activating' particular local groups, the Communist team stimulates a broad range of initiatives both directly and indirectly through anticipatory responses. The mayor of Chelles claimed that consultation had resulted in an increased variety of direct demands on city government, as well as more vocal criticism of decisions that were being considered. The Mayor of Athis-Mons admitted that at least one major decision to establish a center for young school-children had been abandoned in favor of a crêche for infants because of strong communal pressure. By opening up the political process, Communist local governments have found it difficult to avoid the input and the criticism of some groups from which they do not draw political support, particularly where groups are well established, and take seriously the rhetoric about open decision-making. Thus, neighborhood committees in Le Havre and Nîmes pre-dated the establishment of Communist governments in 1965. In both cities these committees have served as on-going participants in the political process and effective critics of the local governments.[47]

Not all local groups have benefited from this dialogue, of course. Clearly, Communist local governments have tended to favor those groups that are closest to the party, particularly committees that have been initiated by the municipality itself. Some local associations have been isolated from the decision-making process either because they are clearly identified with the political opposition, or because they advocate objectives that are not compatible with important aspects of local policy. Thus, for example, an African soccer club in Aulnay was isolated from support by the city government because the deputy mayor in charge of sports opposed 'the reinforcement of racial segregation.'[48]

Other groups have been crushed by Communist local government because they posed an unacceptable political challenge. 'As a general rule, anything that moves on the left and that the communists do not control, is suspect.'[49] While this statement is somewhat exaggerated, since Communist mayors have worked with groups controlled by the Socialists, they have made great efforts to crush groups and associations that they have considered *gauchiste*.

Nevertheless, even the hostile confrontation between Communist local governments and 'unacceptable' groups has often produced contradictory results. For example, groups advocating segregated activities have been opposed by Communist mayors, but the mayor of Poissy was careful to describe the initiation of a 'folklore festival' that emphasized the different traditions of the various immigrant communities in Poissy.

* * *

Directly and indirectly Communist municipalities tend to see local government as a process of coalition-building among groups and sectors of the community. Although, like local governments of the right, Communist local governments have attempted to stabilize their support by dispensing individual services such as a limited number of jobs and apartments in public housing, their approach to coalition-building has been to develop policies and services for those groups that form a part of their target constituency. Therefore, as their view of their constituency has changed, the range of their policy involvement has broadened — from simple aid to working-class families in the early years, to programs for schoolchildren, programs for the aged and cultural services in the late 1960s, to complex decisions about urban development more recently.[50] Thus, like party and inter-party relations, the interchange between Communist local government and various local groups and associations is not only a key element in the process of mobilizing the capacity to obtain benefits from the state, but is also an important element in developing policy initiatives and the will to make demands from the state.

Notes

1. Jacques Duclos, 'Les Municipalités au service des masses laborieuses,' Report to the 14th Congress of the PCF, 1956, p. 101, cited in Ronald Tiersky, *French Communism 1920–1972* (New York: Columbia University Press, 1974), p. 354.
2. Marcel Rosette in *Cahiers de l'Institut Maurice Thorez*, No. 19, 1976, 'Municipalités et luttes politiques,' cited in Raymond Pronier, *Les Municipalités communistes* (Paris: Balland, 1983), p. 70.
3. Ibid., pp. 72–5. Pronier is particularly good at describing the role of the 'canal' for informally transmitting orders.
4. Ibid., pp. 97–8.
5. *Le Monde*, May 19, 1981.
6. *Le Monde*, November 3, 1981.
7. He had been excluded from the section by only two votes in 1981 and had maintained the support of his Communist colleagues on the municipal council.
8. *Le Monde*, March 18, 1983.
9. Pronier refers to this directive on p. 73, op. cit.
10. See Pronier, op. cit., pp. 74–7, for cases in which the party has learned to live with opposition, at least in the short run.

11. Denis Lacorne, *Les Notables rouges* (Paris: Presses de la FNSP, 1980), p. 86.
12. Ibid., p. 96. Lacorne notes, however, that the purpose of this separation is not to increase the independence of the elected official, but to prevent the *accumulation* of significant individual power within the party.
13. Sidney Tarrow, 'Party Activists in Public Office: Comparisons at the Local Level in Italy and France,' in Donald Blackmer and Sidney Tarrow, eds, *Communism in Italy and France* (Princeton: Princeton University Press, 1977), pp. 163–72.
14. See Philippe Garraud, 'Le Recrutement des maires en milieu urbain: esquisse et typologie,' *Pouvoirs*, No. 24, 1983.
15. Pronier, op. cit., pp. 56–64.
16. *Le Monde*, April 12, 1978.
17. See Lacorne, op. cit., p. 95, documented in his fn. 79.
18. *Le Monde*, May 7, 1972.
19. *Bulletin de l'Élu Communiste*, No. 1/2, 1973, p. 10.
20. Marcel Rosette in *L'Élu d'Aujourd'hui*, February 1978, p. 3. Also, see Pronier, op. cit., pp. 87–90. In 1975, the name of the quarterly had been changed from *l'Élu Communiste* to *Communes et Départements d'Aujourd'hui*.
21. Pronier, op. cit., pp. 90–4.
22. *L'Élu d'Aujourd'hui*, June 1978, p. 8.
23. Pronier, op. cit., p. 299.
24. Marcel Rosette, *La Gestion communale dans l'action* (Paris: Éditions Sociales, 1977), p. 200.
25. Pronier, op. cit., pp. 226–8, 382–8.
26. Ibid., p. 303.
27. INSEE, direction générale des collectivités locales, service central des enquêtes et des études statistiques, *Inventaire Communale, 1979–80*; also see Pronier, op. cit., p. 299.
28. Jean Pierre Hoss, *Communes en banlieue: Argenteuil et Bézons* (Paris: Armand Colin, 1969), p. 120.
29. Pronier, op. cit., pp. 105–10.
30. Pronier cites several examples of this. See op. cit., pp. 116–17.
31. See, for example, the reporting on computer training in *L'Élu d'Aujourd'hui*, June 1978, which specifically refers to the fine services rendered by Sigma-formation, which was followed by a half-page advertisement (pp. 50–1) by the same company.
32. Jean Montaldo, *La France Communiste* (Paris: Albin Michel, 1978), pp. 176–9.
33. Pronier, op. cit., 116–17.
34. Jeannette Becquart-Leclercq, *Paradoxes du pouvoir local* (Paris: Presses de la FNSP, 1976), Ch. 3; Also see Jack Hayward, *The One and Indivisible French Republic* (New York: W.W. Norton, 1973), p. 34.
35. However, Stephane Dion, in a study of two Socialist and two Communist-governed cities in the Paris region, found that municipal committees were a more effective instrument for 'calling the minority party to account,' by drawing the minority councillors into a game that

they did not control. Stephane Dion, 'Le Maire de gauche, son parti, sa municipalité,' *Pouvoirs*, No. 24, 1983, p. 77.

36. Ibid.
37. Aubry, mayor of Sevran, April 10, 1978.
38. Jeannette Becquart-Leclercq, 'Les Chemins du pouvoir local: la selection du maire,' *Pouvoirs*, No. 24, 1983, p. 100.
39. Pronier, op cit., p. 348.
40. Rosette, *La Gestion* . . . , p. 40.
41. Ibid., p. 41.
42. Henry Canacos, *A l'Écoute des villes de France*, cited in Pronier, op. cit., p. 209.
43. Hoss, op. cit., p. 123.
44. André Donneur and Jean G. Padioleau, 'Local Clientelism in Post-Industrial Society: The Example of the French Communist Party,' *European Journal of Political Research*, **10**, No. 1, March 1982, p. 78.
45. Pronier, op. cit., p. 212.
46. Hoss, op cit., pp. 125–8; See Pronier, op. cit., pp. 327–34, 350–1, for the various forms of consultation attempted by the Communists.
47. Pronier, op. cit., p. 351.
48. Ibid., p. 352.
49. Ibid., p. 353.
50. Therefore, Communist local governments have been particularly careful to maintain control over associations that dispense concrete services, such as the CNL, the Association of Tenants in public housing development. See Donneur and Padioleau, op. cit., pp. 78–9. However, these authors tend to confuse broad policy with clientelist relations.

6 Conclusion: Local Government and the Communist Experience

In terms of the scope of their objectives, and the structure and process through which these ojectives are developed and achieved, Communist-governed municipalities have been different as a group from those governed by other parties. Unlike other municipalities, they have approached local government as a party effort, both locally and nationally, with the result that there have been striking similarities among the policy choices made at the local level.

Their efforts have emphasized the expansion of such services as education and aid to school children, cultural facilities, the development of public housing, and, more recently, balanced urban planning. Indeed, in these areas Communist local governments have played a ground-breaking role. In contrast to most other local governments of comparable size, Communists have tended to view local government as an arena for policy innovation and change. This emphasis is consistent with their views of legitimacy at the local level, as well as with their strategy for building support.

Clearly, local innovation has not been limited to the efforts of Communist-governed cities, nor have these municipalities alone necessarily been the most innovative in recent years. The Socialist mayors of Grenoble, Rennes and Marseilles all innovated new programs and services during the 1960s that compare favorably with (and by some estimates surpass) those of comparable Communist cities.[1] Dijon, governed by a Gaullist council, became a model of balanced urban development during the 1970s, and Vincennes, with a centrist mayor, developed a broader range of social services than its Communist-governed neighbor, Fontenay-sous-Bois.[2] Moreover, the striking innovations of Communist governments — those that clearly have set them apart from other cities — generally pre-date the 1970s; recent policy departures generally involve expansion of some services and contraction of others, rather than new policy departures.

Nevertheless, what continues to characterize these cities is the similarity of their policies and their commitments as a group. Certainly there are differences among Communist-governed municipalities, but given their social and geographic diversity, the similarities of their *politique sociale* are impressive. What sets them apart is not the determined will of one or several mayors to achieve certain objectives, but a political structure and process that stimulates and supports policy development. This system of interaction, provided essentially by the PCF, is more complex than the model of a party hierarchy would indicate, but it is also more coherent than that provided by any other national party.

We have argued in this study that there is a link between the coherence of Communist-governed municipalities and their historic ability to generate successful programs of services and projects at the local level. The party links, we have argued, both strengthen the will of these municipalities to develop new programs, and diminish their dependency on state services for the initiation of these programs. Thus, party links have historically helped to promote decentralized policy-making (in relation to the state), and more centralized policy-making (in relation to the party). There is no question that the will for the major initiatives undertaken by Communist-governed municipalities has been stimulated and supported by the intra-party system of relations and inter-actions, and that the development of these initiatives has been facilitated by party support services. At the same time that these towns have been less dependent on state priorities, however, they have been more dependent on the priorities of the party.

If for a long period of time party relations were a source of creative local initiatives and innovative policies, the party now appears to be less capable of this kind of stimulation. The older bastions are no longer the models for new departures. This role appears to have been assumed by the towns governed by Communist–Socialist coalitions, where policy initiatives have been stimulated by national and local inter-party competition. Although electoral support has been rapidly eroding in the former towns, it has been generally maintained in the latter towns.

Nevertheless, the ability of Communist-governed towns to develop programs and services focuses our attention on the importance of local will for the augmentation of local government capacity. Before 1981, the access of Communist-governed towns to state decision-making was at best limited and conditional. However, far more than in municipalities governed by other parties, they tended to generate policies that were dependent upon state cooperation for their success. In theory, Communist local governments may have chosen to maximize their autonomy from the central state (and from ministries dominated by parties of the right) by pursuing goals that would depend upon local resources and by mobilizing electoral support on the basis of the 'failures' of the central governments dominated by the right. However, from the very earliest years of Communist local government, they have sought to attract support on the basis of their *réalisations* (achievements) as well as their opposition to the bourgeois state. This orientation has been formed, strengthened and supported by the network of relations within the party and by the competitive pressures that have grown among the parties of the left. Thus, if they have been less dependent upon state services in the development of their initiatives, they have been more dependent than most other municipalities upon state decision-making for their success.

Despite specific instances of political prejudice against Communist-governed municipalities, Communist mayors have been effective in gaining their objectives within the politico-administrative system. They have managed their requests and their 'dossiers' skillfully, and have learned to bargain forcefully with the administration. In fact, it appears that although the administration has been biased against patronage requests, it has been far more open to policy and program requests from Communist local officials than is generally admitted. However, insofar as Communist-governed municipalities have been able to develop a characteristic set of policies and programs, their success is due far more to their will to initiate than to their relative access to the administrative system. Indeed, it appears that their will and commitment have strengthened their access.

The Communist experience illustrates well the ability of local governments in France to initiate and mold policy priorities, even before the 1982–3 decentralization reforms. The Communist pattern, or at least aspects of this pattern, has also become increasingly characteristic of local government in general in France in recent years. As national parties have developed greater coherence and have gained greater control over local political elites, local government personnel and local policy priorities have increasingly reflected the needs and the priorities of national parties.

The 1983 local election campaign demonstrated the growing politicization of local politics in France, among parties of the right as well as the left. The growing interest of the opposition parties in controlling candidate selection at the local level was reflected in the national agreement reached between the UDF and the RPR on January 21, 1983 on which party would head the list in each of the 231 large cities (population over 30,000). They failed to reach agreement in only five of these cities. Moreover, each party devoted considerable energy to enforcing the agreement by pressuring local notables into conformity. In Strasbourg a former RPR minister, André Bord, was forced to run as the head of a dissident list when the RPR decided to constitute a united list with a UDF head; in Metz, the RPR candidate withdrew in favor of the UDF-led united list.

In the Paris region, particularly the four departments of the outer ring where centrist mayors have been dominant for generations,

> departmental headquarters of the parties of the right have taken things in hand. They and only they certify candidates. And if the 'inheritors' of the former bosses . . . have played an important role in the preparation of these municipal elections, it has been as much as men of the party as [in their capacity as] presidents of the general council. It is out of the question, in any case, for the Union of the Yvelines or for the Union for the Seine-et-Marne [departmental organizations for the right opposition] . . . to give any certifications beyond those accorded by the RPR and the UDF. The label of union, so sought after, even in the small communes, can

> only come from the common support of the two great forces of the opposition . . . That curious situation that separated the general councillors of the RPR and the UDF between the group of Union for the Essonne and that of 'non-inscrits', according to the personal contacts of each mayor is finished. Partisan structures have put everyone in their place, even if some of the most established elected officials regret the [loss] of their former 'freedom.'[3]

The 'non-inscrits' (those candidates who are not formally designated by a political party) were not obliged to join one of the parties of the right, but they were constrained to conform to criteria established by the RPR and the UDF at the department level. Through threats and hard bargaining, the two major parties were able to control the composition of united lists in the Paris region.

Although the RPR and the UDF were not successful in reaching agreement on a national electoral program, the UDF itself agreed to a 'Municipal Manifesto' in November 1982. This vaguely worded document that proposed more criticism of the Socialist–Communist national government than proposals for municipal policy nevertheless implied that local government was party government, and its rhetoric echoed the notion of a 'contract,' first used by the left:

> These six commitments constitute for us, the candidates of the UDF, a contract that we establish with the French [electorate]. We call on them, with us, to make our communes into windows of democracy. They foreshadow what will become of the nation tomorrow when the power is returned to it.[4]

These actions by the parties of the right (similar to those taken by the Communists long ago and by the Socialists a decade ago) have generally put to rest the notion of 'apolitical' elections, even among voters in the smaller towns. When voters were asked in 1970 if the municipal elections would be 'political' in their town, only 19 percent responded that they would. By 1977 the same question evoked positive responses among 62 percent (and half of those who responded from the smallest rural communes); in 1982, 73 percent gave a positive response to a similar question. Similarly, when voters were asked if their electoral decision was related either to the policy of the president (in 1965 and 1977) or to the policy of the national government (in 1983), a positive response was given by 30 percent in 1965, and 44 and 50 percent in 1977 and 1983.[5]

There is some indication that the electoral cooperation of the right has been carried through into coordinated policy choices at the local level. This was most evident in the widespread campaign against cultural services carried out during the months following the 1983 municipal elections in a large number of cities 'reconquered' by the right. In more than a dozen cities previously governed by popular front coalitions, there were systematic closures of *maisons de la culture*, dismissals of personnel directing cultural services, and the abrogation of contracts for 'cultural action.'[6] For the first time, the RPR named a national delegate for cultural affairs (Jean-Claude Groshens, a former president of the Pompidou Center), whose responsibility was to coordinate municipal cultural action. This coordinated action was generally justified, by Groshens and others, as a necessary reaction to the widespread politicization of these services by the left, particularly the Communists, during the period in which they had governed.[7]

The RPR has also begun to develop regular contacts among their mayors. Although their political orientation is certainly different from that of the left, their approach to the local government process is a conscious reaction to the Communist model. Thus, at a reception for new RPR mayors at the Paris city hall on May 10, 1983, Jacques Chirac was reported to have said that the new mayors 'should show themselves generous in the social and cultural areas, in order to prove their ability to do better than the Communists and the Socialists.'[8]

Therefore, recent events seem to indicate that the Communist pattern of local government is neither exotic nor unique. Indeed, the pattern appears to be increasingly characteristic of local government in general. Local policy-making has become increasingly important, and has become increasingly linked to national party networks. Moreover, many of the policy choices of governments of the right, are either reactions to or emulations of services developed in Communist-governed municipalities. We can reasonably conclude that Communist-governed cities have been different from those governed by other parties. They will certainly be less different in the future in terms of their process of policy development. Whether the content of their policies will be different will depend on the ability of the PCF to renew its commitment to innovation and change.

Notes

1. See Mark Kesselman, 'The Tranquil Revolution at Clochemerle: Socialist Decentralization in France,' in Philip Cerny and Martin A. Schain, *Socialism, the State and Public Policy in France* (London: Frances Pinter, 1985); and Jack Hayward, *Governing France: The One and Indivisible Republic* (London: Weidenfeld and Nicolson, 1983), Ch. 2; and D. Bleitrach, J. Lojkine, E. Oary, R. Delacrois and C. Mahieu, *Classe ouvrière et social-démocratie: Lille et Marseille* (Paris: Éditions Sociales, 1981).
2. Raymond Pronier, *Les Municipalités communistes* (Paris: Balland, 1983), p. 235.
3. *Le Monde*, February 15, 1983.
4. Le Monde, *Les Élections municipales de mars, 1983* (*Supplément aux documents du Monde*, 1983), p. 27.
5. *Sondages*, Nos 3–4, 1977, pp. 86–7, and Nos 2–3, 1978, p. 85; as well as Jean-Luc Parodi, 'Dans la logique des élections intermédiares,' *Revue Politique et Parliamentaire*, April 1983, p. 46.
6. *Le Monde*, July 9–10, 17–18, 24–5, 27, 1983.
7. *Le Monde*, July 24–5, 1983.
8. Ibid.

Index